Counterinsurgency in Eastern Afghanistan 2004–2008

Memoirs and Occasional Papers Series
Association for Diplomatic Studies
and Training

Series Editor: Margery Boichel Thompson

In 2003, the Association for Diplomatic Studies and Training (ADST), a nonprofit organization founded in 1986, created the Memoirs and Occasional Papers Series to preserve firsthand accounts and other informed observations on foreign affairs for scholars, journalists, and the general public. Through its book series, its Foreign Affairs Oral History program, and its support for the training of foreign affairs personnel at the State Department's Foreign Service Institute, ADST seeks to promote understanding of American diplomacy and those who conduct it. U.S. Foreign Service officer Robert Kemp's account sheds light on both the civilian and military aspects of civil-military cooperation in counterinsurgency and on the resources in time, people, and money devoted to achieving allied goals in Afghanistan.

OTHER TITLES IN THE SERIES

Claudia Anyaso, ed., *Fifty Years of US Africa Policy*
Diego and Nancy Asencio, *The Joys and Perils of Serving Abroad: Memoirs of a US Foreign Service Family*
Janet C. Ballantyne and Maureen Dugan, eds., *Fifty Years in USAID: Stories from the Front Lines*
John Gunther Dean, *Danger Zones: A Diplomat's Fight for America's Interests*
Robert E. Gribbin, *In the Aftermath of Genocide: The US Role in Rwanda*
Allen C. Hansen, *Nine Lives: A Foreign Service Odyssey*
Joanne Huskey, *The Unofficial Diplomat*
David T. Jones, ed., *The Reagan-Gorbachev Arms Control Breakthrough: Eliminating Intermediate-Range Nuclear Force (INF) Missiles*
John G. Kormann, *Echoes of a Distant Clarion: Recollections of a Diplomat and Soldier*
Armin Meyer, *Quiet Diplomacy: From Cairo to Tokyo in the Twilight of Imperialism*
William Morgan and Charles Stuart Kennedy, eds., *American Diplomats: The Foreign Service at Work*
John David Tinny, *From the Inside Out*
Daniel Whitman, *A Haiti Chronicle: The Undoing of a Latent Democracy, 1999–2001*
Susan Wyatt, *Arabian Nights and Daze: Living in Yemen with the Foreign Service*

For a complete list of series titles, visit <adst.org/publications>

Counterinsurgency in Eastern Afghanistan 2004–2008

A Civilian Perspective

Robert Kemp

MEMOIRS AND OCCASIONAL PAPERS SERIES
ASSOCIATION FOR DIPLOMATIC STUDIES AND TRAINING

Washington, DC

Copyright © 2014 by Robert Kemp

New Academia Publishing/Vellum Books 2014

The views and opinions in this book are solely those of the author and do not necessarily reflect those of the Association for Diplomatic Studies and Training, DACOR, Inc., or the Government of the United States, including the Department of State.

All rights reserved. No part of this book may be reproduced or transmitted in any form or by any means, electronic or mechanical, including photocopying, recording, or by any information storage and retrieval system.

Printed in the United States of America

Library of Congress Control Number: 2014946564
ISBN 978-0-9904471-4-6 paperback (alk. paper)

 An imprint of New Academia Publishing

 New Academia Publishing
PO Box 27420, Washington, DC 20038-7420
info@newacademia.com - www.newacademia.com

All photographs in this book were taken by the author

For Kate and Kiara

Contents

Foreword by Ronald E. Neumann	ix
Preface	xiii
Acknowledgements	xvii
Acronyms and Foreign Terms	xix
1. Introduction	1
2. Strategy and Strategic Goals	17
3. Insurgent Groups	23
4. Civilian Components	27
5. Local Government	31
6. Development and Reconstruction	47
7. Security	69
8. The Role of Provincial Reconstruction Teams	83
9. The Afghanistan-Pakistan Border	99
10. Nangarhar Case Study: Progress in COIN and Counternarcotics	111
11. The Rise of Radical Islam in the Border Areas	127
12. Analysis of RC-East	135
13. Conceptual and Strategic Considerations in RC-East	149

Annexes	159
Annex I: The District Program (DDP): A Case Study in Organizational Challenges	161
Annex II: Khost Province in 2004-2005: A Case Study	175
Annex III: Three Case Studies in Civil-Military Cooperation as a Function of Security, 2004-2005	191
Annex IV: Position of PRTs on the Civil-Military Spectrum, 2004-2005	199
Notes	207
Index	219

Foreword

America was attacked from and went to war in Afghanistan in the first year of the twenty-first century. Nearly midway into the second decade Americans are winding down only their own participation; the war continues. With but a few exceptions, writings about the war have focused either at the policy level or on aspects of combat and the military. Americans are vaguely aware that civilians also served; particularly diplomats, aid workers, contractors, and civil servants from numerous cabinet departments, including Agriculture, Justice, Homeland Security, State, and others. But as to what these many civilians did, risked, and tried to accomplish few in the general public could say. When journalists or inspectors occasionally criticize, they often do so with no discussion of why decisions were made or with any understanding of either the challenges or reasons for action. This is not to argue against the view that many mistakes were made; they were. In general that is the story of all wars, particularly irregular wars fought in strange surroundings that need to be learned even as events demand decisions before learning can take root.

Against that background Robert Kemp's work fills in many blank spots about the civilian side of civil-military cooperation in counterinsurgency. It is the personal account of a Foreign Service officer who was prepared to return several times to Afghanistan to serve his country. That in itself is a story of service that exemplifies many American diplomats and their civilian colleagues and is much too little appreciated by those who still hold a striped pants and teacup view of what it means to be a diplomat.

Kemp's work focuses on Eastern Afghanistan in the period 2004 to 2008, part of which occurred during my time as US ambassador to Afghanistan. It was a period generally marked by under-resourcing, particularly in civilian personnel, some of which resulted from the flow of resources to Iraq. Much of it however, derived from the hollowing out of American diplomacy during the previous twenty years, when administrations of both parties thought they could do with either less diplomacy or fewer people to carry it out. The frequent reference in the book to staffing gaps and responsibilities that exceeded any reasonable grasp were a direct result of the massive personnel shortages that the American Academy of Diplomacy documented in 2008.[1] Our war efforts paid the price for this neglect. We should not repeat the experience.

The reader will find certain themes recur through the book. Progress early on was strong; but as the insurgency picked up speed, much of the progress was reversed. In examining this trend in Eastern Afghanistan, the area covered by Kemp, two facts are particularly important. One was that much of the impetus for the increase in fighting came from across the Pakistani border. The other was that American inputs did not keep pace with the change. In April 2007, in my last major report before leaving post, I noted that while we were not losing then, we could be in a year, and we had no margin for surprise.[2] This book deals with parts of the field-level work that gave rise to that analysis.

Another recurring theme is that of the harmful results of our short-tour policies. Military and civilian personnel come for a year or so and depart. Knowledge is lost, plans are changed (often to the confusion of Afghans who remain), focus is shifted before efforts have put down solid roots, and the increasingly disgusted locals have to reeducate the foreigners every few months. Until we are prepared to keep senior personnel in place for considerably longer tours we will not succeed in building a learning organization to deal with complex local realities.

Lack of sufficient, trained Afghan bureaucratic personnel was a continual roadblock. That was simply a fact of life. It needed long-term training over many years to reverse the effects of twenty-five years of war and the near-total destruction of Afghanistan's educational system. Some of that training is now happening; but those like Robert Kemp who worked in the early years simply had to live with the problem. No amount of concepts and coordinating structures could wholly make up for the absence of people—something to remember when evaluating the results of that period.

As the insurgency worsened, we increased our security—"force protection," in the jargon. The result, as Kemp notes, was to reduce the mobility of our personnel and their interaction with Afghans, which in turn, reduced our local knowledge and ability to refine our actions. Clearly, the result was lost effectiveness. More recently, after the politicization of the losses in Benghazi, this trend has considerably worsened. We have not always been this risk-averse. We operated on quite different principles in Vietnam. If the current trend continues, so will the reductions in knowledge essential for intelligent policy.

A particularly interesting development in the later part of Robert Kemp's time was the effort to shift the focus of aid and governance from a provincial to a district level, at least for districts deemed key to the war effort. Kemp's description of that shift is a usefully detailed account of the enormous resources in time, people, and money that were required to move from concept to effective implementation. This is an important lesson for those who think success is just about getting the policy right.

In war, as my military colleagues used to remind me, "the enemy gets a vote." That is particularly apparent in the many cyclical developments recorded here—areas where there was considerable progress that then slipped for various reasons. In some cases progress was restored. In others the task will now be up to the Afghan government. Kemp's discussion of Nangarhar is telling. It was one of the brighter provinces for a time. Much of that progress has been lost; local power brokers are challenging the once powerful but now ailing governor, crime is on the upswing, as are opium poppy production and insurgency. Some of the problems stemmed from the lack of follow-through on aid promises. Many are purely local issues. All is not lost, but the swings remind one that in a counterinsurgency progress is rarely linear and needs constant reinforcement.

It is clear that some efforts failed during the period of this work. Others succeeded only in part. And some made a real difference.

While judging the results is important, it is important also to understand how new, complicated, and difficult the times and circumstances were. Much had to be learned the hard way, by trial and error, when time precluded lengthy study and knowledge was slight. We should not lose either the knowledge gained of how to operate in such circumstances or our understanding of how difficult it was to acquire that knowledge. To both those ends this work makes a real contribution.

Ronald E. Neumann
U.S. Ambassador to Afghanistan 2005–2007

Preface

After the attacks of September 2001, the United States found itself rapidly engaged in combat operations in several areas of Afghanistan, notably the plains and hills north of Kabul and the western areas around Kandahar. After quick victories there, the United States and its international allies expanded their presence, including into the eastern quarter of the country. Eastern Afghanistan was and is a remarkable place – a land of high mountains, Islam, complex tribes, nomads, poppy growing, tradition and honor, war and hospitality, multiple layers of history, rapid social change, and startling beauty. This book looks, in part, at what happened in the early years of a new century when the United States encountered eastern Afghanistan.

Focus of the Book

The purpose of this book is to provide a civilian perspective of the U.S. engagement in eastern Afghanistan during 2004–2008, particularly in terms of counterinsurgency (COIN) and its many facets. Afghan society was changing rapidly, and the insurgency was transforming itself, making this effort even more complex. A somewhat ad-hoc U.S. government organizational structure evolved into one where interagency responsibilities and coordination were better defined, while civilian-military relations became more organized and balanced, resources were increased, and new strategies and tactics were put in place. Different cultures and personalities played a role in policy and operations; personal relationships were key.

The Government of Afghanistan was slowly beginning to gain form and function at the national and local levels, and the Afghan Army and police forces began to assert themselves under the new government. International players, including Pakistan, India, and other neighbors became involved in ways that added to the situation's complexity, often creating difficulties for counterinsurgents.

Sources and Methods of Research

Much of the book draws on the author's experiences on the ground in Afghanistan. These included a posting from 2004 to 2005 as the political advisor for the 1st Brigade of the 82nd Airborne Brigade Combat Team (ABCT), headquartered in Khost Province along the border with Pakistan, and concurrently as the political officer at the Khost Provincial Reconstruction Team (PRT). During a second posting from 2007 to 2008, the author was attached to the 173rd ABCT headquarters in Jalalabad, again bordering Pakistan and served as the lead officer for local government at the U.S. Embassy and as the deputy director of the PRT section. The author was assigned to the Interagency Provincial Affairs section within the U.S. embassy in the spring of 2010, working on a program to provide local governance and development immediately after combat operations. While in Washington, the author was the deputy director of the Pakistan desk and also did three short-term assignments in Pakistan. In Brussels, the author was a political-military officer assigned to the U.S. Mission at NATO from 2005 to 2007.

Sources include interviews—both publicly available and those conducted by the author—with other State Department and military officers who served in Afghanistan during this time and with their counterparts in Washington. Afghan sources were used, as well as open-source articles and publicly available U.S. government documents.

Book Format

The first four chapters introduce the area covered by RC–East, the actors involved, and their goals and strategies. Chapters five through seven look at the main "pillars" of counterinsurgency: security, governance, and development. Chapters eight through eleven look at two case studies, one a tool (PRTs) and the other geographic (Nangarhar Province), as well as two major factors: the nature of the Afghan-Pakistan border and the nature of Islam along this border. The last two chapters analyze what happened during this period and draw lessons learned.

Four annexes at the end of the book look in detail at specific programs, areas, and efforts to make complex organizations work.

Besides the two case studies mentioned above, others case studies look at efforts to strengthen local governance through the District Delivery Program (Annex I), operations in Khost province (Annex II), and maneuver battalion operations in Bermal, Paktika province, a UN program to bring stability to a difficult area, and elections (Annex III).

While many military aspects of the U.S. counterinsurgency effort in Afghanistan have been thoroughly reported in both open-source articles and internal U.S. government documents, analysis of the civilian aspects is less comprehensive. This book is meant to fill part of this gap. At the same time, views of the Afghan government and civilians are largely underrepresented in the Western press, enough so that this book intends to break new ground in this area.

This study is one person's perspective, informed by various participants, including the U.S. government, the Government of Afghanistan, the Government of Pakistan, the United Nations, nongovernmental organizations (NGOs), the various insurgent groups, and the views of the different branches of the U.S. military. Most of the chapters draw on the author's views of what happened and why and include lessons learned. It was written with military and civilian officers in mind—those who need to make policy succeed in the field—but in hopes that it will be of interest to other readers who have a general interest in what happened in Afghanistan during this time and why. It is also written to document hard-won knowledge that too often was lost when officers and units rotated out of Afghanistan.

Acknowledgements

While this book focuses on a four-year period of the war in Afghanistan, in the end it took much longer than that to write, and the author is indebted to many people as a result.

I would like to thank the soldiers, Marines, and Special Forces of the U.S. military for getting me "outside of the wire" on two year's worth of patrols, battlefield circulations, and development trips. Afghanistan can be a difficult and, at times, dangerous place to move around in, but these professionals set high standards and kept to them. I also benefited from their views on COIN, civilian-military relations, and Afghanistan. Similarly, this book has benefited from conversations with many State Department, USAID, and USDA officers, along with the dedicated men and women of NGOs and the United Nations.

A special thanks to Robert "Turk" Maggi, twice Political Advisor at the headquarters in Bagram, for his unique brand of insight, strategic overview, and outrageous sense of humor. Dennis Hearne, also a Political Advisor, contributed with insights gained over several tours. Several outstanding military officers, including then Col. Patrick Donahue, LTC Mike Fenzel, Major (Reserve) Carl Hollister, and Col. Chip Preysler and his talented staff helped a civilian understand more about the military tribe.

Afghanistan is also a complex, and rapidly changing country. This book is a reflection of conversations with many Afghans—civilian and military, both in and out of government—during my time in their country between 2003 and 2010. Theirs is a wonderful country, and I thank them for their efforts to explain it.

Parts of this book were initially published, in somewhat different versions, in various journals: *Military Review*, the *Georgetown Journal of International Affairs*, the *Small Wars Journal*, the *SAIS Bologna Center Journal of International Affairs*, and the military journal *Campaigning*. I would like to acknowledge their permission to reprint these articles.

Many thanks to Georgetown University's Institute for the Study of Diplomacy, where parts of this book were written during a year as a Dean Rusk Fellow, funded by the U.S. State Department. Also at Georgetown, thanks to Alba Seoane, for her skills as a research assistant, and to the students in my spring 2012 class on Afghanistan, for bringing new perspectives and criticisms to a complex situation.

The Association for Diplomatic Studies and Training adopted my book in its series and shepherded it to publication. Special thanks to Margery Thompson, ADST's publishing director and series editor, for skillfully and patiently transforming a draft manuscript into a book, and to ADST interns Brianna Guarino and Mary Edwards. Several anonymous reviewers looked at earlier drafts and thereby improved the final product.

Thanks to Jane Ann Kemp for reading and commenting on the many drafts of the articles that formed the basis for much of this book, as well as the draft manuscripts of the book.

And to Shiela, for holding down the home front during frequent absences in Afghanistan and Pakistan over a decade, and for giving me the space to write.

I appreciate the concurrence of my employer, the U.S. Department of State, in the publication of this book. However, the views expressed herein do not represent those of the U.S. government, the U.S. Department of State, the Institute for the Study of Diplomacy, or the Association for Diplomatic Studies and Training; they are my views alone.

Acronyms and Foreign Terms

ABP	Afghan Border Police
ADT	Agribusiness Development Teams
AID	U.S. Agency for International
alberkai	tribal militias raised to provide security for specific events or emergencies
ANA	Afghan National Army
ANDS	Afghan National Development Strategy
ANP	Afghan National Police
ANSF	Afghan National Security Forces
AO	Area of Operations
ARG	Afghanistan Reconstruction Group
ASOP	IDLG's Afghan Social Outreach Program
AVIPA	USAID's Afghanistan Vouchers for Increased Productive Agriculture program
BCCs	Border Coordination Centers
BMTF	Border Management Task Force
CAT-A	Civilian Affairs Team – Alpha
CERP	Commander's Emergency Response Program
CENTCOM	US Central Command
CJSOTF	Combined Joint Special Operations Task Force
CJTF	Combined Joint Task Force
CMOC	Civil-Military Operations Center
CN	Counter Narcotics
COPs	combat outposts
COIN	Counterinsurgency
CSTC-A	Combined Security Transition Command -Afghanistan
CT	Counterterrorism
CTF	Combined Task Force
DAS	Deputy Assistant Secretary of State
DAI	Development Alternatives Inc.
DDP	District Development Program
DDR	Disarmament, Demobilization and Reintegration

DIAG	Disarmament of Illegally Armed Groups
DST	District Support Teams
EU	European Union
FATA	Federally Administered Tribal Areas (Pakistan)
FMF	Foreign Military Funding
FOBs	forward operating bases
GAO	U.S. General Accounting Office
GoA	Government of Afghanistan
GDP	Gross Domestic Product
GPI	Good Performers Initiative program
HDI	Human Development Index
HiG	Hezb-e Islami Gulbuddin
ICMAG	Integrated Civil-Military Action Group
IDLG	Independent Directorate for Local Governance
IED	Improvised Explosive device
IJC	ISAF Joint Command, charged with running day-to-day ISAF operations
INL	State Department's Bureau for International Narcotics and Law Enforcement (INL)
IO	information operations
IO	International Organizations
IOM	International Organization for Migration
IPA	Interagency Provincial Affairs
ISI	Pakistan Inter-Services Intelligence
KTD	Key Terrain District
LOCs	lines of communications – usually major roads and highways
MAIL	Ministry of Agriculture, Irrigation and Livestock *meshrano jirga* upper house
MoI	Ministry of Interior
MRRD	Ministry of Rural Rehabilitation and Development
NABDP	UNDP's National Area-Based Development Program
N2KL	Nangarhar, Nuristan, Konar, and Laghman provinces
NDS	National Directorate of Security
NGO	nongovernmental agencies
NSC	National Security Council

NWFP	North West Frontier Province
ODAs	Operational Detachments 'A"
ODBs	Operational Detachments "B"
ODHACA	Overseas Humanitarian Disaster and Civic Aid
OEF	Operation Enduring Freedom
PRTs	Provincial Reconstruction Teams
PTS	Takhim – e –Sol Program, or the National Program for Reconciliation
QAQC	quality assurance/quality control
RAMP-UP	USAID Afghan Municipality Support Program
RC-East	Regional Command East
RoL	Rule of Law
shuras	assemblies
SCR	Senior Civilian Representative
S/CRS	State's Office of the Coordinator for Reconstruction
S/SRAP	State Department of the office of the Special Representative for Afghanistan and Pakistan
TF	Task Force
TIC	troops in contact
TOC	Tactical Operations Center
UAE	United Arab Emirates
UNAMA	United Nations Assistance Mission To Afghanistan
UNDP	United Nations Development Program
USDA	United States Department of Agriculture
USG	United States government
USFOR-A	U.S. Forces Afghanistan
wolesi jirga	lower house

1

Introduction

Overview of the Border Regions of Eastern Afghanistan

The Afghan frontier remains a wild and colorful place, still tied more to what Kipling saw in the late nineteenth century than to the modern world. With the attacks of 9/11 and the resulting U.S. military intervention in Afghanistan, America—and its NATO allies—found themselves engaged in a very foreign land, culturally complex, often violent, while at times strikingly hospitable. A kaleidoscope of issues—history, Islam, foreign influence, money, drugs, land, personalities, and arms—came together to make this engagement exceedingly complex. This made it difficult for foreigners to see any sort of "big picture" clearly. At the same time, the (re) entry of the outside world into a conservative, often closed, traditional society certainly was a shock to the Afghans, while being a source of hope as well.

The insurgency and counterinsurgency in eastern Afghanistan involved a complex range of players and factors. These include ethnic and tribal groups; Afghan, U.S., and Pakistani security organizations; and political and religious leaders. In turn, the nature of the insurgency varied from province to province, and even district to district. This book will examine in detail the various factors that influenced counterinsurgency (COIN) during this period. The next sections offer a general overview of the history, culture, and geography of the military zone covered by Regional Command-East (RC-East), with subsequent chapters focusing on particular topics.

History of Afghanistan since 1979: A Series of Wars

Viewed during the years immediately following the U.S.-led overthrow of the Taliban, Afghanistan had suffered a tremendous amount of physical damage, inflicted by twenty-five years of war on an already minimal infrastructure. Much of Kabul was ruined, highway bridges on the major routes out of town were destroyed, public services were minimal to non-existent, and the population was generally exhausted. This was the result of five periods of warfare with almost no intervening periods of peace. The first period was the Soviet invasion, when uprisings against the government, notably in Herat Province in western Afghanistan and in Konar Province in the east, were followed by the deployment of the Soviet 40th Army in December 1979. This war lasted ten years, reaching its height in 1985, when the Soviets made a final major push to win the war—while also devastating the countryside in a counterinsurgency strategy based on forced depopulation.[1] The results of this strategy can be seen to this day, not only in the Afghan refugees still living in Pakistan and Iran, but in destroyed irrigation systems, numerous minefields, and ruined villages.

The second period of warfare pitted the Communist regime of President Najibullah against the mujahedeen groups formed to fight the Soviets, ending in 1992 with the collapse of his regime. Following this was a period many Afghans remember as worse than the Soviet war: the fighting between the various mujahedeen factions. This civil war resulted in the destruction of much of Kabul, particularly West Kabul, areas of which remained in ruin in 2004. Partly in reaction to the resulting anarchy, a fourth period of fighting ensued, with the Pakistani-backed Taliban beginning operations in Kandahar Province in November 1994, and subsequently advancing to capture Herat and eventually Kabul. Finally, the fifth, period of war began with the U.S.-sponsored defeat of the Taliban and al-Qaeda in late 2001.

Following the October 2001 invasion by the U.S.-led coalition, the nature of the conflict along the border changed and evolved. After clashing with Coalition forces—including a battle in the Shah-i-Kot area of Paktia province— al-Qaeda and much of the Taliban leadership fled into Pakistan. There followed a period during which local strongmen struggled for power, while the coalition

Introduction 3

Map of Afghanistan and Surrounding Countries

Source: Central Intelligence Agency
Accessed: http://www.lib.utexas.edu/maps/middle_east_and_asia/txu-oclc-309295540-afghanistan_pol_2008.jpg, *August 2012*

and Afghan government also acted to increase their control. After appearing largely defeated, the Taliban and associated insurgents intensified their operations in the border provinces beginning in the spring of 2005, mostly thorough an increased quantity and sophistication of improvised explosive devices (IED) strikes but also through coordinated attacks on patrols, indirect fire attacks on bases, propaganda campaigns, and attacks on pro-government and pro-coalition Afghans.

Geography of RC-East:

The area of eastern Afghanistan covered by RC-East, included 13 provinces, from Nuristan in the north to Paktika Province in the south, and northwest to Bamian Province, then west to Daikundi (later split off from RC-East) The city of Kabul was in its own military zone, and RC-East commands had limited activity in the province of Kabul during this time.

The climate ranges from intense winter cold and heavy snow in Nuristan and other highland areas to oppressive heat and humidity during the summer in Nangarhar and Khost. In RC-East ,temperatures range over the year from more than 20 degrees below Fahrenheit to 130 above. Many areas are nearly desert, although monsoons at times reach this far north, bringing rain to dry areas. These rains and the spring thaw often result in localized flooding, particularly given the deforestation in many areas.

The scarcity of water in many parts of RC-East is a fundamental factor. Average annual precipitation in Gardez is 8.6 inches, in Jalalabad 9.7 inches, and in Bamian only 5.5 inches [2] Irrigation sys-

Map of Regional Command East and Adjacent Pakistan

tems are key to agriculture, and determine where much of the rural population lives. Several rivers – the Konar, Kabul, and Khost rivers - have large volumes of water year-round. Other streams are intermittent or flow into salt pans, and many areas are covered in rock, sand and thick dust.

State and Social Disintegration

Although the physical damage resulting from the wars beginning in 1979 was what immediately struck any outsider, conversations between the author and Afghans from various social classes during the 2003-2008 period made it clear that the damage to society was even more extensive. First was the sheer number of people killed, with more than one million Afghan civilians losing their lives in the war against the Soviets[1] out of an estimated population of sixteen million in 1979.[4] Equally striking were the masses of refugees, with more than five million displaced,[5] mostly to Iran and Pakistan, but also to Europe, North America, and Australia.

More subtle damages were the cleavages within society, primarily along ethnic lines. In some areas, such as Khost Province in the east, deep divisions existed between those who sided with the Communist regime and those who fought with the mujahedeen. The Taliban years also left social rifts between those who fought with the Taliban and those (particularly in Tajik and Hazara areas) who opposed them. Adding to this is the fundamental disturbance to the tribal system, particularly in the Pashtun areas where it had been both a local government and a source of stability. On a larger scale, the last twenty-five years of Pakistani involvement in Afghan affairs had caused considerable resentment and suspicion on the part of Afghans.

Social Structure in RC-East

While the violence and dislocations of the last decades certainly had a strong impact on Afghanistan, the cultural constants that held the Afghans together still remained. Foremost was Islam, which reached every corner of society, and was an immensely strong influence at both the individual and community levels. The role of families was also very strong, along with kinship units. In Pashtun areas the "Pashtunwali" cultural code remained, and provided strong behavioral norms and social frameworks.

These were tough people, physically resilient, often willing to use violence, and often courageous (a bravery it seems in part driven by social norms and expectations, but also perhaps by deep religious beliefs and the reality of short lifespans). Gender separation was often stark, particularly in rural areas, where women spend much of their time in family compounds. Rules governing women's behavior were often strict, especially in rural areas, and could be harshly enforced.

A significant percentage of the population had been displaced internally or externally by wars since 1979, adding another stress on this society, and many had spent time in nearby refugee camps in the Federally Administered Tribal Areas (FATA) or near Peshawar. As the Pakistani government closed the camps across from RC-East during this period, thousands of refugees cross the border, often on short notice. While the Government of Afghanistan (GOA) and Coalition would scramble to respond, extended families and tribal networks often absorb these populations.

The series of wars beginning in 1979 had, by 2004, exhausted much of the population in the border areas, which was probably bordering on collective post-traumatic stress disorder. This fatigue presented opportunities to both sides—whoever could provide stability and an end to the violence had a chance to win popular support. Security was most people's highest priority—including protection from insurgents, thieves, militias, and enemy tribes, not to mention corrupt security forces. Economic prosperity—jobs and income—was a close second.

Ethnic Groups

The main ethnic groups in RC-East were Pashtuns, Tajiks, Hazaras, and Nuristanis, with some smaller groups including the Peshaei. Along the border areas, the Pashtuns were by far the largest group, with the Hazaras in the central highlands, the Nuristanis in the far northeastern part of the country and the Tajiks further north away from the border (see map). Some of these groups, particularly in the cities, were ethnically mixed, and often spoke more than one language. The Kuchis, a mostly Pashtun nomadic group that migrated between Pakistan and Afghanistan looking for pasture for their animals, often caused friction with the settled populations. Where the lands of these ethnic groups met – particularly where Hazara and Pashtun groups came together —there were often tensions.

Tribes remained strong in some areas, particularly the Pashtun areas in Khost, Paktika, Paktia and Nangarhar. There were a bewildering array of tribes and sub-tribes with often contentious complex relations between themselves. Many of these border tribes claim swaths of territory on both sides of the frontier, and move across at will. In others areas tribal influence had waned, due to historical, social or cultural factors, or had never been strong to begin with. The world of the border tribes was changing rapidly, as improved roads, communications, and increased government involvement came to the area. Clearly, understanding the people was vital to winning the counterinsurgency and to developing sustainable political and economic institutions.

Generalized Ethnic Divisions within Regional Command East and Adjacent Pakistan

Afghans' View of Coalition Forces

The border populace was generally receptive to Coalition forces during this time. Afghans, to some extent, viewed these forces as a stabilizing presence that kept Afghans from fighting other Afghans, particularly at a tribal level. They also saw coalition forces —in the form of maneuver battalions or PRTs as distributors of projects and aid in areas where international organization (IO) or Government of Afghanistan (GOA) projects did not reach. Underlying this support was a deep concern that anarchy will return if Coalition forces were to leave.

Interestingly, many Afghans remembered the U.S. involvement in the jihad against the Soviets and saw the United States (and by extension U.S. troops) and Afghanistan as two countries bound together by war. At the same time, they viewed Americans as being religious people, as opposed to the (as viewed by Afghans) atheistic Soviets.

In contrast, most Afghans in the border areas—through all levels of society— viewed Pakistan as an enemy. They considered Pakistani involvement in the insurgency a clear and obvious fact, and remembered the recent Pakistani backing of the Taliban. They perceived coalition forces, through their presence, as deterring Pakistani meddling.

Islam in RC-East

Islam influences almost all facets of Afghan life and is a basic foundation of society. Even the smallest towns have mosques, and farmers in their fields stop for prayer wherever they may be standing. Historically, Islam has helped unify Afghanistan and the Afghans. Roughly 85 percent of the country is Sunni; the remainder is Shiite.[6] In RC-East, the Hazaras were the largest Shiite group; most of the remainder of the population was Sunni. Tolerance between the two groups as well as Hindus, was the pre-1979 norm. The traditional form of Islam in Afghanistan, while tremendously influential in society, is not particularly radical, although there was heavy social pressure to conform to norms—including the conversion of the Nuristanis to Islam in the 19th century. It also appears to have only minimal hierarchy within RC-East, instead having independent local leaders. Although influences from the Deobandi school of the subcontinent, as well as Wahhabist and Salafist thought from the Arab world have made inroads, the traditional version remains predominant. Sufism is also practiced, and Sufi leaders such as Pir Gailani have both spiritual and political influence in border regions.

Increased Influence of Mullahs

The influence of mullahs and other religious leaders increased in recent decades in RC-East, according to many Afghans, some of whom described mullahs as previously being tolerated more than venerated. Magnus and Naby[7] explained the traditional role of the mullah as "a man who led the prayer, presented a sermon on Fridays especially, recited or read from the Koran, officiated at life-cycle services, adjudicated disputes, and taught boys how to read the Koran." By 2005 in –RC-East, there was a split in the ranks of the mullahs, with a minority supporting the Taliban and its ideology, and a more moderate majority supporting the Afghan government. This split resulted in violence, with attacks on and assassinations of moderate mullahs.

Economy and Development

Afghanistan was and is one of the poorest countries in the world—the United Nations Development Program's (UNDP's) 2004 report on Human Development Index noted that "Afghanistan's [2002] HDI value of 0.346 falls at the bottom of the list of low human development countries, just above Burundi, Mali, Burkina Faso, Niger, and Sierra Leone."[8] Life expectancy in 2002 was just over 44 years, and national literacy rate was just above 28% (but only 14.1 percent for females), one of the lowest among developing countries. Adjusted per-capita GDP was only $822. Particularly in the rural areas of RC-East, the general lack of basic services and the meager gains from subsistence farming could be shocking to outsiders from developed countries. While these numbers improved by 2008, clearly this very low baseline was a challenge for development workers and counterinsurgency efforts.

Much of the population in RC-East is rural, subsisting on irrigated crops and livestock, while the towns support small shopkeepers and limited light industry. Overall, poverty is endemic, and even the most well-off towns are far from wealthy.

At the national and international levels, the Interim-Afghanistan National Development Strategy (I-ANDS and eventually the ANDS) and the Afghanistan Reconstruction Trust Fund provided overarching frameworks. However, these plans were just being implemented during this period, and local Afghan officials as well as coalition officers were often not well informed about them. The "lead nation" concept was agreed to at the Tokyo donor's conference in 2002, designating individual nations with responsibility for a specific developmental area (for example the Italians were to lead on justice, and the Germans on the police). However, such designations generally did not translate to activity by these nations on the ground in RC-East.

General Overview of Government

The general structure of local governance had been established over previous decades, although the series of wars had caused already weak structures to deteriorate. In theory, the Afghan government is a strongly centralized system, with power mostly flowing from Kabul. In practice, the central government had limited influence in much of RC-East, due to lack of financial and human resources, corruption and inefficiency, and the inherent difficulty of governing the border regions and its people. Roles and responsibilities were defined in law, although in practice it was often ad hoc, driven by personality, and varied considerably between and within provinces. The relationship between the central government in Kabul and the provinces was not always clear and often depended on personal relationships.

At the top of the local political hierarchy were the provincial governments, headed by governors, appointed directly in Kabul for open-ended terms. Ministries' representatives for provinces reported to Kabul, and were not accountable to the governor. The district governors, also appointed, the only officials the majority of Afghans ever met, were on the bottom rung of governance. Municipal government was ill defined in many ways, covering both urban and rural areas of varying sizes. Elections in the fall of 2005 chose members of the provincial councils, as well as members of the *wolesi jirga* (the lower house); members of the *meshrano jirga* (upper house) were indirectly elected.

During this period, the Afghan Government at all levels—national, provincial, district, and municipal—was undergoing a slow and difficult process of reestablishing itself. Rebuilding (or building) government in the middle of an insurgency, with limited human and financial resources, was difficult, and tribes and communities often provided governance where the reach of the formal government did not extend. At least on paper, Afghanistan has one of the world's most centralized governments, which put control of development planning and funding in the ministries in Kabul. At the same time, the ministries were "stovepiped," with lines of authority extending directly to officials of that ministry in the provinces, often bypassing governors' or mayors' offices.

Pakistan's Influence on the Border Areas

RC-East shares a long border with Pakistan, mostly the North West Frontier Province (NWFP, later renamed Khyber Pakhtunkhwa) along with a small border with Baluchistan in the south. The Federally Administered Tribal Area (within the NWFP) fronted much of this roughly 1500 kilometer shared border. Much of the actual border was the Durand Line, drawn by the British in the late 1800s and never accepted by the Afghan Government. This line effectively divided the Pashtun populations in both countries, although in many places, it was more a line on a map than a firm border dividing two countries, with people and goods flowing across with only limited regulation. The reality of a largely artificial border dividing the Pashtuns, coupled with closely related and linked insurgencies on both sides of the border, meant that events in Pakistan had a very direct impact on RC-East (see chapter 9 on the Afghan–Pakistan border for a more detailed discussion).

12   *Counterinsurgency in Eastern Afghanistan*

Meeting between U.S. soldiers and local Pashtun leaders to discuss development projects. Afghan interpreter to left, in black fleece jacket and hat. Paktika Province, winter of 2004.

Introduction 13

Meeting with local men to discuss U.S. presence and development programs. Pesh Valley, Konar Province, 2004.

Irrigated fields and family compounds seen from the door of a helicopter. Khost Province.

Border between Khost Province, Afghanistan, and North Waziristan, Pakistan.

Houses and fields in Hazara area, Bamian Province, 2005.

2

Strategy and Strategic Goals

In broadest terms, the strategy of the Government of Afghanistan (GOA) was reflected in the Afghan National Development Strategy, adopted in 2008. This had as its main goals:

1. Security: Achieve nationwide stabilization, strengthen law enforcement, and improve personal security for every Afghan.
2. Governance, Rule of Law and Human Rights: Strengthen democratic practice and institutions, human rights, the rule of law, delivery of public services and government accountability.
3. Economic and Social Development: Reduce poverty, ensure sustainable development through a private sector-led market economy, improve human development indicators, and make significant progress towards the Millennium Development Goals.[9]

In general, U.S. COIN strategy in RC-East paralleled the GOA's strategy, with a three- "pillar" approach that included 1) economic development, 2) security and 3) governance.[10] Counternarcotics and information operations were subordinate but important elements. Rule of law (which could be included under the governance pillar) and counterterrorism (CT) (which could be included under security) were also major elements of the strategy.

U.S. strategy was driven and limited by the resources available, with the Afghanistan theater clearly secondary to Iraq. For example, in 2004 RC-East was covered by only one brigade,[11] along with some special operation forces and PRTs. U.S. strategy had both CT and COIN aspects to it,[12] and this balance shifted over time, and with different commanders. At the same time, higher strategy was adapted and modified to fit local conditions by field-grade officers. In general, the military used a shape-take-hold-build strategy for field operations.

During the early part of this period, Combined Forces Command-Afghanistan (CFC-A), the overall command of U.S. forces including those in RC-East, had this mission statement: "conduct full spectrum operations throughout the combined joint operations area to defeat al-Qaeda and associated movements, establish an enduring Afghan security structure and reshape its posture for the Long War in order to set the conditions for long-term stability in Afghanistan." This command mandated three main lines of effort for Operation Enduring Freedom (OEF): security; economic and strategic reconstruction; and governance and justice. The desired end-state of CFC-A was, "A moderate, stable and representative Afghanistan capable of controlling and governing its territory."

By 2007–8 additional troops were available in RC-East. These additional resources allowed for smaller bases and combat outposts to be established, moving forces off the larger bases and closer to the population. This made sense in terms of securing the local population from attacks or intimidation by the insurgents, an important factor in counterinsurgency. But it added to the logistical problems of supplying outposts in remote areas, particularly during the winter months; moreover, these outposts were vulnerable to enemy attacks.

By early 2009, the U.S. Military reported to Congress that "The strategic goals of the U.S. are that Afghanistan is: 1) never again a safe haven for terrorists and is a reliable, stable ally in the War on Terror; 2) moderate and democratic, with a thriving private sector economy; 3) capable of governing its territory and borders; and 4) respectful of the rights of all its citizens."[13]

UNAMA Strategy and Responsibilities

The Security Council originally delegated a range of responsibilities to the United Nations Assistance Mission in Afghanistan

(UNAMA), in particular managing relief, recovery and reconstruction, holding elections, and providing strategic advice to other actors such as the U.S. military. This has the ultimate goal of promoting peace and stability in order to achieve national reconciliation. UNAMA's role in RC-East specifically was (and is) to implement the UN's political strategy of Afghan relief, reconstruction, and development, with particular concern for the maintenance of schools and commitment to the completion of construction projects.

Insurgent Strategies

The insurgency was composed of several different groups with different goals. A UNAMA political officer based out of Gardez during this time, Sebastian Trives, accurately describes the strategy of the insurgent groups in RC-East:

> Prevent government outreach by estranging the population from it. This is done through the intensification of propaganda, the targeting of government personnel and infrastructure, and the creation of an atmosphere of fear within communities fueled by intimidation as well as acts of violence and killings targeting individuals seen to be pro-government.
>
> Continue to target the international presence, both civil and military, in order to limit its operational space in the short term, while at the same time augmenting the political costs of involvement for the governments of the main contributing countries.[14]

The Haqqani network, an important insurgent group in eastern Afghanistan, intended to "force the departure of Coalition forces, primarily in their territory of Loya Paktia (the provinces of Paktika, Khost, and Paktia) through sustained harassment and persistent attacks aimed at creating an atmosphere of instability."[15] In assessing the group's current goals and projected activities, this same source indicates that the Haqqanis may also "seek to strengthen their negotiating position ahead of any reconciliation talks" and "may in fact be angling for de-facto control of the Southeast;" in addition, the group wants to increase its influence in Logar and Ghazni in order to attack nearby Kabul, and control part of Route 1 that runs between Kabul and Kandahar.

Throughout the period 2004–2008, the insurgents were establishing shadow governments and justice systems, co-opting some tribes, establishing bases within Afghanistan, expanding the areas where they could operate, and hindering development projects. The ultimate goal of the Taliban was to regain control of Afghanistan. The next chapter will examine the various insurgents groups in RC-East in detail.

Strategy and Strategic Goals   21

Men and boys in Khost town, 2005.

Aerial view of a typical Pashtun village, Khost Province, 2005.

3

Insurgent Groups

The insurgency in RC-East was neither monolithic nor easily understood. Terms such as "anti-coalition militias" or "al-Qaeda and associated militias" were used by the United States as catch-all phrases, but were not particularly useful in defining an insurgency composed of many factions. The number of players involved in the insurgency also did not allow an easy analysis of the goals of the insurgency, other than a general intent of forcing the Coalition out of Afghanistan, toppling the GOA, seizing power, and forming an Islamic state.

Along the frontier with Pakistan, the insurgency included not only the Taliban but also al-Qaeda, the Hezb-e- Islami Gulbuddin (HIG) of Hekmatyar, foreign jihadists, perhaps Pakistani extremists groups, and fighters associated with Jalaluddin Haqqani – a former minister in the Taliban government. The motivation and goals of these organizations differed, but with some overlap and probably some degree of coordination between the groups. At the same time, not all of these groups were active in all border areas – Hekmatyar operated more in Konar and Nangarhar, while Haqqani's network focused on Khost, Paktia, and Paktika, later reaching to Kabul.

In some cases, money rather than ideology drove attacks on coalition or Afghan forces as in the case of a poor farmer receiving money from the Taliban to set off an IED; similarly, some attacks may have been related to the narcotics business. In other cases, Afghans in remote areas were hostile to outsiders in general, and would take pot-shots at any intruders into their valley. This complex situation at times made it difficult to know what adversary had initiated an attack and for what reason – and by extension– made it more difficult to develop an effective counterinsurgency strategy.

Geographic Variations of the Insurgency

Besides varying from an ideological standpoint, the insurgency varied geographically between provinces. In Paktika, Khost, and Paktia Provinces, much of the insurgent violence was ideological in nature, with groups crossing the border from Pakistan in small groups, carrying out attacks, and then retreating into North and South Waziristan, in the FATA.

In Konar Province to the north of Jalalabad, the situation was even more complex. Apolitical violence was commonplace, not only because of the lucrative earnings to be made in smuggling drugs, timber, and jewels, but because of a high level of common crime. At the same time, ideological groups from Pakistan could easily cross the border to carry out attacks on Afghan and coalition forces, as well as the GOA. The rugged topography of Konar attracted insurgents, who established a base of operations in the Korangal Valley, west of Asadabad, in the summer of 2005. Similarly, some insurgent elements in Konar and Nuristan had a Salafi/Wahhabist element that was strongly ideological, and had been present for years.

Taliban as the Leading Force of Insurgency

The Taliban was the largest and most important of the groups composing the insurgency during this period. It could be viewed in two, overlapping ways: as an ideological organization, committed to spreading a conservative view of Islam; and as an ethnic Pashtun organization—one that promoted Pashtun interests.

In general, the Taliban had limited support among the border population for a variety of reasons. The locals viewed Taliban attacks on security forces and pro-government Afghans as a cause of further instability and violence, in a population that badly wanted peace and stability. While the influence of Islam in the border region was tremendously strong, permeating every facet of life, the strict views of the Taliban were out-of-sync with much of the population, particularly younger people who had lived outside Afghanistan. The Taliban discredited itself through the mismanagement of government while in power, particularly by neglecting administrative functions; many rural areas were self-governing during the period 1997–2001. Finally, they were seen as linked to Arab extremists like al-Qaeda, which some blamed for some of Afghanistan's problems over the previous decade.

Across the border in Peshawar, many educated Pashtuns had a more benign and supportive view of the Taliban. They saw the Taliban as promoting and protecting ethnic Pashtuns from threats, be they from other ethnic groups, governments, or military forces. Others continued to view the Taliban as a pious and devout Muslim group, a protector of moral values, although this appeared to change by 2008 as the Taliban increased its operations in Pakistan.

While the Taliban could carry out disruptive attacks, they had limited ability to operate in large groups for long periods. They were overmatched in any fight against Coalition forces and increasingly so against the Afghan National Army (ANA). In 2005, their tactics centered on IED attacks, minor attacks on patrols and bases, and the intimidation and assassination of GOA officials and pro-government mullahs. Interestingly, they rarely carried out attacks that would kill large number of civilians – like rocketing cities. Their inability to disrupt the September 2005 Parliamentary elections and the October 2004 Presidential elections reflected limited capabilities, but may also have reflected a narrow understanding of elections, their importance, and how to subvert them. However, by the end of this period, the Taliban and other groups were showing some success as measured against their strategy (as outlined at the end of Chapter 2). By carrying out attacks, or maintaining the threat of attacks, they certainly decreased the ability of local government and the Coalition to do their jobs, and drove a wedge between some local communities and the government.

Other Insurgent Groups

The network of Jalaluddin Haqqani claimed responsibility for a considerable number of attacks in Khost, Paktia, and Paktika Provinces during this period, and was perhaps the most formidable opponent in these provinces, particularly as it gained strength. Operating out of North Waziristan, Haqqani, a former mujahedeen leader and his commanders (including his son Sirajuddin Haqqani, who increasingly took over leadership from his aging father during this period) at times mustered forty or more men for cross-border attacks, several of which were repulsed with many casualties after coalition forces called in air strikes. The goals of these attacks may have been for propaganda purposes – to show that his network was capable of attacks on military, as opposed to civilian, targets. At the same time, if fighters were receiving training in Pakistan, these may have been "graduation" exercises. The group also increased their ability to carry out IEDs and suicide bombings. The Haqqanis had ties with the Zadran tribe, which controlled an area at the intersection of Khost, Paktika and Paktia Provinces; these links increased their ability to operate inside Afghanistan. They also expanded their capacity to attack as far away as Kabul during this period.

The roles of other insurgent groups were less clear. al-Qaeda issued statements denouncing the coalition presence in Afghanistan, and may have been behind some car bombings. Several al-Qaeda leaders were detained or killed in the FATA, suggesting an active engagement in the insurgency. Public statements by the Pakistani military noted that sweeps in the FATA often encountered Arabs, Chechens and Uzbek fighters. HIG had actively opposed the GOA, and the coalition presence and may also have been responsible for some attacks in Konar and Nangarhar.

Pashtun Population as the "Center of Gravity"

During 2004 and 2005, much of the insurgent activity in eastern Afghanistan was in three border provinces – Paktika, Khost, and Konar – with lesser but still significant activity in the southern districts of Ghazni, and along Paktia's border with Pakistan. Not coincidentally, this area – roughly southeast of the country's ring road – has a predominantly Pashtun population, where the Taliban found some degree of support and could blend more easily into the local population. In the struggle for "hearts and minds," these Pashtuns were the center of gravity for both coalition forces and the Taliban and its associated militias. Further to the north and west, the ethnic composition of the population had a larger percentage of Tajiks and Hazaras, which made it much more difficult for the Pashtun-based Taliban to operate effectively. Due to this ethnic composition, these areas experienced a lower volume of attacks.

4

Civilian Components

This section will look at the roles of the various U.S. and international civilian actors in RC-East during the period 2004–2008, as well as some perspective from Washington.

State Department Political Officers

The State Department assigned political officers to both the PRTs and the Brigade HQ. These officers had four main tasks. First, they were reporting officers, tasked to provide information on political, political-military, economic, and social trends to the Embassy in Kabul. Second, they were conduits of information to the U.S. military on various topics: what U.S. government (USG), State Department, and embassy policy was, what was happening in Afghanistan at the national level, and developments in Pakistan—a very relevant topic for the border provinces. Third, they were charged with promoting USG policies to the provincial government. Finally, and in some ways most importantly, they were responsible for helping the nascent GOA govern effectively. At both the PRT and Brigade levels, the political officers traveled with the commanders, meeting with political leaders (usually governors) as well as military leaders. This freed the commanders to focus more on military aspects.

U.S. Agency for International Development (USAID)

USAID officers, called Field Program Officers, were assigned to both PRTs and Brigade commands in RC-East. These officers were responsible for administering USAID projects at the provincial level (although they were not responsible for administering at the provincial level national-level programs run out of Kabul). They were also tasked with advising military officers on development issues; advising the GOA on long-term reconstruction and development strategy, and reporting back to AID headquarters in Kabul. In provinces where NGOs and IOs were present, the AID officers worked with them to assure projects were complementary, and to coordinate development strategy at the provincial level. Unlike the State Department, the AID officer at the Brigade HQ managed the AID workers at the PRTs. Many AID workers at this time were contractors, rather than career employees.

U.S. Department of Agriculture (USDA)

USDA officers focused on providing agricultural advice to the GOA, and to a lesser extent, individual farmers. They were not present in most RC-East PRTs, although two key posts—the Brigade HQ and the Jalalabad PRT—included them. The USDA officers complemented AID counternarcotics programs, providing advice on crops to substitute for poppy and micro credit programs for farmers.

A View from Washington

The State Department's Deputy Assistant Secretary (DAS) for Afghanistan during much of this time described his primary concern as acquiring the necessary "manpower, money, and time."[16] This reflected what he and others saw as the USG's loosely held view that "in Iraq, we do what we must, in Afghanistan we do what we can." In his view, while Gen. Barno clearly wanted to implement a COIN strategy early in this period, the lack of resources made this difficult in practice. At the same time the International Security Assistance Force (ISAF) was not comfortable with COIN, although by 2006, this was the de-facto strategy. The former DAS noted the relative autonomy he and his National Security Council (NSC) counterpart had on Afghanistan policy, since the administration was mostly focused on Iraq policy. This also allowed Embassy Kabul considerable input to policy, and embassy analysis and advice carried weight in Washington.

United Nations Assistance Mission to Afghanistan (UNAMA)

In RC-East, UNAMA had hub offices at Gardez and Jalalabad. The lead political officers worked closely with USG political and military officers. The UNAMA officers had a wide mandate, dealing with conflict prevention and resolution, monitoring human rights, and promoting GOA capacity. They also played a substantial role in organizing elections. The overall approach of UNAMA in Afghanistan was one of a "light footprint" which placed Afghans in decision-making roles with international actors as advisors. This sideline method was presented as the most effective means of ensuring a sustainable and independent government in Afghanistan.

Now that the major players in RC-East and their goals have been introduced, the next three chapters will look at the major pillars of the counterinsurgency strategy: local government, development, and security.

5

Local Government

This chapter will examine how the GOA worked to build up local governance in RC-East during this time, and how the Coalition supported these efforts. The primary focus early in the period was on provincial-level government; only later was more attention paid to the district and municipal levels.

While local governance made progress during this period, it did not receive as many resources as the other two COIN pillars of security and development. In part, this was the result of an imbalance between civilian and military capacity in RC-East, with the military vastly overshadowing the civilian presence, both U.S. and international, including UNAMA. The situation also reflected a limited Afghan ability to absorb assistance, as many of the local government institutions had atrophied over years of war. It was also the result of the priorities in the fight against the Taliban and other insurgent groups, with establishment of adequate security necessary before civil institutions could take root. Building local governance was inherently a slow process. Decades of war had reduced the pool of civil servants, many of whom had migrated to Pakistan or other countries.

A decimated education system made it difficult to produce trained local leaders. Added to this was the lack of infrastructure; in 2004, most governors occupied compounds, but they lacked basic equipment and staff. At the district level, conditions were worse.

Critical Role of Governors

While local Afghan politics is complex, with many formal and informal players, the governor was in most cases the most important political actor in a province. President Karzai directly appointed governors, and to some extent, the governor was Karzai's "envoy" in the province. However, the governor's power varied, depending on his access to funding, his influence with tribes and business groups, his lineage (family history often carried weight), his role in the fight against the Soviets, his ties with the Kabul government, and his speaking and leadership abilities.

Governors were the chief political contacts for coalition military and political officers from 2004 to 2008. They played a key role in the success (or failure) of counterinsurgency efforts at the provincial level. Conversely, support from coalition officials was often critical to the success (and to some extent, the survival) of governors. In RC-East, coalition officers met almost daily with provincial governors to discuss events, coordinate development projects, review security efforts, plan for upcoming VIP visits, review policy guidance from Kabul, or examine potential points of friction in local society.

Several governors in RC-East were successful, notably Mangal (as governor of both Paktika and Laghman), Jamal in Khost, Wahidi in Konar, and Taniwal in Paktia (until his assassination). These governors established reputations for strong leadership, the ability to work well with the local tribes, physical courage, and ties to Karzai. Assadullah in Ghazni, despite allegations of misconduct, brought strong leadership (to the point of leading militias against Taliban forces). Governor Sarobi, the only female governor in Afghanistan, brought national experience and integrity to Bamian. Through their popular support, they opened opportunities for provincial reconstruction teams and maneuver units to engage more with the people, move additional development funding into communities, and push back against insurgents (particularly those from outside of the provinces.) These governors depended heavily on the United States to provide security and development assistance, while U.S. forces depended on the governors to manage the complex politics of their provinces. On the other end of the spectrum, one governor of Konar was replaced after credible reports of corruption and smuggling, one governor of Logar had a minimal impact, returning to his home in Kabul every evening, and one previous governor of Khost had credible allegations of unethical land deals brought against him.

Given the internal divisions in many Afghan provinces, governors played an important role in resolving or reducing tribal or ethnic disputes. For example, Ghazni Province includes Pashtuns, Hazaras, Tajiks, and during warmer months, nomadic Kuchis. Their ethnic differences have historically led to considerable friction, which a skilled governor could help minimize. Tribal and subtribal disputes over land or historic grievances are also potential flashpoints, and the Taliban uses these disputes to their tactical advantage, as they did in the 1990s when they took over much of the country; this is an important consideration when planning any COIN campaign in Afghanistan.

Some governors were important in solving problems that occurred when foreigners interacted with Afghan society. These problems ranged from the benign, such as cultural misunderstandings, to the important, such as crops and property damage during raids, to the critical, when air strikes mistakenly killed civilians. The governors had to walk a fine line between getting the truth out (the Taliban had become expert at distorting the truth regarding coalition attacks) and not appearing biased in favor of outsiders.

In a larger sense, the governors played a critical role in strategic communications, given the cultural complexities, the difficulty (for foreigners) of learning Afghan languages, the deep-seated suspicions towards outsiders, and Taliban disinformation campaigns. Low literacy rates and the isolation of many rural communities made this task even harder. However, many of the governors were impressive public speakers and capably presented the provincial and national government's views and supported coalition efforts. Radio networks helped the government connect with the population, and large *jirgas* (assemblies) presented similar opportunities. For example, in 2007, hundreds of tribal elders attended a shura in Paktika Province, giving Governor Khpalwak a chance to reach much of the province, directly or indirectly.

Governors also played an important role in communicating with decision makers and populations in ISAF home countries. For example, the U.S. embassy sponsored several successful trips by delegations of governors to the United States and Europe, where they presented the "ground truth" of their provinces and described the repressive and violent nature of the Taliban insurgency. This was especially important in Europe, where public support for ISAF efforts in Afghanistan was often shaky. Some governors were also effective in briefing visiting officials, including U.S. congressional delegations.

Several governors played an important part in the 2005 parliament and provincial council elections. They helped organize the elections and explained to a population largely unfamiliar with elections and democracy what the elections were about, why they needed to participate, and what to expect from their representatives after the elections.

Coalition Support to Governors

Brigades, PRTs and battalions helped the governors overcome various obstacles. Brigades hosted regional governors' conferences that brought together governors, their staffs, Kabul-based officials, and provincial security officials to discuss security and development issues. These conferences were useful in comparing notes, increasing communication between governors, and developing regional policies and projects. They also presented opportunities for press briefings. Some PRTs took the lead in arranging for governors to travel to Kabul to meet with embassy and government officials and donor agencies such as the World Bank. The meetings helped the governors better understand the often-complex world of international assistance, while giving donors insights from the field.

Coalition efforts helped governors succeed in other ways. Governors often took credit for coalition-funded development projects, which increased their standing among the people. In more dangerous provinces, military assets—including convoys and helicopters—provided mobility for government officials, and the PRTs helped fund some governors' staffs and train them in basic administrative tasks. The provincial coordination centers, established with coalition support as emergency call centers of a sort, gave citizens points of contact for Afghan security forces. PRT officers, in particular, acted as neutral advisors—giving governors advice that they might not get from locals with personal agendas— while also giving some governors warnings when corruption, favoritism, or bad policy decisions threatened to undermine their credibility with the local population.

Governors as a COIN Liability

Being an Afghan governor during this period was a daunting task, as many provinces had fractured societies, dire poverty, no infrastructure, and active insurgencies. Some governors were not up to the task. The governor of Ghazni, newly appointed in the spring of 2008, had difficulties running his large, ethnically divided and often-violent province and was soon replaced. Counterinsurgency efforts in Ghazni suffered due to the weak administration under this governor and the lack of continuity as governors changed. The long-term absence of many governors from their provinces was a recurring problem, as they spent weeks or months in Kabul or overseas. (One governor in RC-East was relieved for this reason in early 2008.) This was particularly troublesome when their reluctance to delegate authority to deputies caused provincial administration to grind to a halt. Other governors suffered from lack of legitimacy because they had played a particularly bloody role in previous fighting in Afghanistan, or they favored one tribal or ethnic group over another. Some had no resources to provide basic services or got little or no support from Kabul.

Corrupt governors were one of the biggest obstacles to long-term coalition success in RC-East, undercutting counterinsurgency efforts. For example, between 2004 and 2005, the local population in Konar believed that the governor and some provincial security chiefs misappropriated government funds and engaged in smuggling of timber and gemstones. During the same period, the locals saw the governor of Khost Province enriching himself through the sale of publicly owned land. These governors decreased the legitimacy of the Afghan government, provided openings for the Taliban to increase its influence, and almost certainly reduced the credibility of the Coalition forces that worked with them.

Corruption of Afghan officials was a central, recurring theme in conversations with locals during this period.[17] Afghans expected coalition forces to end corruption among provincial officials, and were not at all understanding when this did not happen. They assumed that the coalition lacked the will to counter corrupt officials, or worse, that the coalition accepted the corruption. In fact, both Department of Defense and State officers confronted provincial officials with charges of corruption when they had compelling evidence of its practice, and this may have modified the officials' behavior in some cases. At the same time, mullahs, business groups, and later provincial councils continued to publicly and privately accuse provincial officials of corruption. While some of these accusations clearly had a basis in fact, others may have been fabricated to further the interest of the accusers. Not all of the corruption at the provincial level was destined for the officials' own pockets: some governors used illegal tolls on highways and border crossings to fund projects and the day-to-day running of their governments.

Obviously, corruption existed in Afghanistan before this period, for a variety of reasons. The legal system was never particularly strong, patronage systems were a political reality, and foreign aid—be it from the Soviets or the U.S. beginning in the 1950s, or support for the mujahedeen in the 1980s – provided officials with a potential source of money. The repeated cycles of war, the influence of warlords, and narcotics trafficking also weakened societal norms and made operating outside of the law more acceptable.

Lack of Human Resources

Afghanistan lacked the human capital to fill all governor slots adequately, and Kabul had to scramble to find good candidates willing to work in difficult and dangerous provinces. In some cases, governors had to stay on longer than they wished or to the point of exhaustion. Several governors told me they wanted to leave their posts, but President Karzai had asked them not to. Weak or absent staff support and the lack of facilities or security for the governors' families made the situation worse. In addition, many governors had conflicts or rivalries with other officials in their province, some of whom reported directly to superiors in Kabul, not to the governors.

District Governance

Subordinate to the provincial level of governance are the districts, headed by district governors (also called sub-governors). By law, Kabul appoints district governors, but in practice the provincial governors appointed many of them during the period 2004–2008. In RC-East, district governance varied from being effective to almost nonexistent, and in most cases, the district governors struggled with inadequate funding (they had no budgets of their own) and staffing. The district governor was important because he was the only official presence many Afghans came in contact with, and he and his staff determined how a rural country perceived the government. In most cases, the district centers also had a district police chief. Ministries and judicial authorities were also present in some districts.

The district governors often seemed to merely react to what was happening in their districts, rather than work to accomplish a list of established goals. According to governance advisors Sarah Lister and Hamish Nixon, the district governor's responsibilities often included "dispute resolution and other problem-solving activities depending on relations with the provincial authorities and local, customary, and informal power-holders."[18]

Security and District Governance

From 2004 to 2008, the availability of resources, the level of security, and the insurgent threat determined district government effectiveness. Security also affected the coalition's ability to support district governance; within RC-East, the ability of insurgents to hinder district governance ranged from negligible in Bamian Province to very significant in Nuristan, Konar, Khost, and Paktika Provinces.

The coalition reacted to security conditions at the district level with a variety of responses. In 2004 in Paktika Province, the 2nd Battalion, 27th Infantry (2-27 IN), under Lieutenant Colonel Walter Piatt, deployed groups of soldiers, usually led by captains, to district centers for weeks at a time. This provided enough security for the nascent district governments to begin to take root, gave the officers an opportunity to mentor and work with Afghan officials, and provided U.S. forces a good picture of what was happening on the ground. This program worked, in part, because the insurgent groups were only just organizing in Paktika. (In contrast, when British forces in Helmand Province first deployed to district centers, Taliban forces quickly pinned them down, and they faced considerable logistical challenges.) The Bermel District of Paktika, across from Pakistan's South Waziristan Agency, suffered from constant attacks; insurgents had twice overrun the district government. To counter this, in 2005 the U.S. 1st Battalion, 508th Infantry Regiment, based in Paktika Province, established a firebase that also served as the district center.[19]

The security situation in Khost Province gradually worsened from 2004 to 2008, as insurgent groups, particularly the Haqqani network, increased their capabilities. Initially, civil affairs team members from the PRT and company commanders from the maneuver battalion based in Khost supported district officials by visiting their compounds during daylong patrols. By 2007, the security situation dictated that most of the district centers be fortified and guarded by soldiers and police. In parts of Konar and Nuristan Provinces, particularly the Pesh, Korangal, and Waygal Valleys, localized insurgencies were strong, hindering the growth of local governance and even threatening firebases. An insurgent attack on Wanat in July of 2008 left nine U.S. soldiers dead.

On the other hand, security in Nangarhar Province improved so much that by 2008, Afghan security forces took over much of the responsibility for the province. District-level governance expanded due to the efforts of the Jalalabad PRT and a special troops battalion, which ran forward operating bases and patrol bases in several of the districts.

Shortcomings and Suggestions

While State Department political officers posted to the PRTs and the brigades visited the district centers, their limited numbers meant that most support went to provincial governments. More civilian focus at the district level later bore fruit. (In 2009, the U.S. embassy in Kabul posted officers at the district level.)

Elections of district governors had been under consideration several times but had not yet occurred. During the 2005 provincial elections, the international community judged that holding simultaneous district level elections made the mechanics of the elections too complicated. District governor appointments were sometimes handed out as favors, and some appointees reportedly enriched themselves in districts with smuggling routes.

Additional Government Institutions

Provincial councils and the municipalities were two other important layers of local governance, although coalition forces worked with them less often than with the governors and district governors. Elections in September 2005 chose members of parliament and provincial councils. The councils' first task was to pick one of their members for the meshrano jirga. Beyond this task, their job was less defined; involvement in developmental planning, environmental protection, and evaluating provincial government seemed to be common themes.[20] Limited funding often hindered their effectiveness.

The Independent Directorate for Local Governance

The Independent Directorate for Local Governance (IDLG) was established in August 2007 by Afghan presidential decree, with the mandate to "consolidate and stabilize, achieve development and equitable economic growth, and to achieve improvements in service delivery through just, democratic processes and institutions of governance at the sub-national level, thus improving the quality of life of Afghan citizens."[21] The Ministry of Interior (MOI) had previously been responsible for sub-national governance, but it had acquired a reputation for corruption and inefficiency. Nationwide, the IDLG inherited more than 10,000 employees of varying quality and abilities; however, its core staff—those formulating and implementing national policy—appeared to number less than 100 in the spring of 2008.

The IDLG represented a fundamental shift in how Kabul administered local governance, and it had immediate implications for COIN strategy in RC-East. The directorate took a much more vigorous approach to managing local governance than the MOI had. At the same time, IDLG officers began to assert themselves as the supervisors of local officials. They demanded a say in how PRTs, battalions, and brigade staffs related to local governments, and asked that Kabul be informed of coalition interactions with provincial officials.

With considerable support from President Karzai and the international community, the IDLG began an ambitious program to overhaul governance at the provincial, district, and municipal levels. It also began increasing its influence in Kabul and improving coordination with other ministries, some of which had considerable stakes in local governance. An important step forward was the development of the "Five Year Strategic Work Plan" in April of 2008. The plan outlined general goals including policy development, institution building, and broader governance, nested within the overarching Afghan National Development Strategy. A coherent and realistic document conceived with support from international advisors, the plan laid out a blueprint for local governance and described areas where donors could provide financial and technical assistance.

Challenges Facing the IDLG

As with all previous Afghan governments, the IDLG faced the difficult task of extending its writ to the provinces. This was a daunting task, given the size of Afghanistan and its rugged terrain, harsh winters, and the lack of a transportation infrastructure. Additional challenges included limited resources, several governors who acted quite independently, the need to balance complex political situations at both the national and local levels, and the need for President Karzai to become involved in decision-making at the local-governance level. Added to this were very real security considerations for those traveling in parts of the country.

A major hurdle for the IDLG was the lack of trained civil servants—a result of decades of war, of the migration of a significant percentage of the population to other countries, and of an education system that, by 2001, was almost nonexistent. Some of the best governors were those who had returned from overseas, but significant security risks, hardship, and low pay kept others away, a situation even more evident at the district and municipal levels.

In the IDLG's favor was the remarkably rapid expansion of cell phone coverage to many parts of the country and the availability of internet service in cities; such capability allowed the directorate to be in almost constant communication with many governors. Commercial air travel was gradually becoming available for cities such as Herat, and the Afghan military's air wing began flying to more places, allowing IDLG officers to visit the provinces more easily.

Beginning in late 2007, the directorate began a review of provincial governors, removing some of the more corrupt and inefficient ones. Criteria for new governors included loyalty to President Karzai, the ability to work with the local population, administrative and governance capabilities, and the ability to work with the coalition. Some of the newly appointed governors were marked improvements, particularly Wahidi in Konar Province. One of Afghanistan's best governors, Mangal, was moved from Laghman to the strategically important province of Helmand to address the daunting counternarcotics and counterinsurgency challenges in that province. In the spring of 2008, the directorate began reviews of its Kabul staff, as well as mayors and district governors.

Transfer of Authorities to the Provincial Level

The IDLG, as part of an effort by several ministries, began to redraft local governance laws and policies. This included examining how to devolve power from Kabul to the provinces to give local officials greater budgetary and policy authority. From a COIN perspective, this had the advantage of making local government more responsive to its constituents, but in Kabul, there was some resistance to giving more budgetary authority to governors, because it could decrease the influence of ministries that channeled funding directly to their offices in the provinces. The transfer of power to the local level had the potential of giving more Afghans input into government programs and policies, moving decision- making to a level where it could adapt to local conditions (an important consideration in a country as diverse as Afghanistan), persuade people that a government is in place and functioning, and counter Taliban shadow governments.

However, compelling historical and practical reasons argue against devolution of power to the provinces. In the past, some governors have become powers unto themselves, with little accountability to Kabul. Others have come under the influence of neighboring countries, or become local warlords or the proxies of local warlords. As noted, governors in some ways act as the Afghan president's envoy to a province, so Kabul has an interest in maintaining control over them, particularly during the run-up to elections. History has also shown that Afghanistan has the potential to fracture along ethnic or regional lines, which is an argument for maintaining power in Kabul.

The current constitution leaves open the option of some devolution of power. Article 137 of the constitution says, "The government, while preserving the principle of centralism, shall delegate certain authorities to local administration units, for the purpose of expediting and promoting economic, social, and cultural affairs, and increasing the participation of people in the development of the nation."[22]

An important factor in the long run will be the development of a civil service cadre with enough officers available to run government effectively at the local level. At the same time, a strong center will also need to remain in place to hold Afghanistan together. As World Peace Foundation president Robert Rotburg notes, "Regardless of ethnicity, many Afghan politicians and policymakers from across the country favor a strong central state in order to curb powerful regional figures who often receive support from outside the country, as well as to reduce the danger of criminal influence over local government."[23]

The U.S. military and the PRT office (which also had access to helicopters and aircraft) helped the IDLG with transportation to the provinces, where provincial officials, who rarely received visitors from the central government, treated the visits as major events. The governors often assembled dozens of provincial leaders, including district governors, provincial council members, security chiefs, and tribal leaders for roundtable discussions; they held smaller meetings focused on governance, security, and development. These trips yielded positive results not only as consultations, but also as demonstrations that the central government was extending its reach to the provinces. Still, a considerable disconnect remained between the center and the provinces.

A fundamental problem for Afghan governors was the lack of funding for the day-to-day operation of provincial government and discretionary projects or emergency responses (an important consideration in Afghanistan, with its droughts, floods, and earthquakes). The IDLG approached the international community in early 2008 to help establish a "governor's fund" to provide money directly to governors with a reputation for honesty and efficiency.

Government Lessons Learned from RC-East:

As the U.S. Army/Marine Corps Field Manual *Counterinsurgency* notes, "Success in counterinsurgency operations requires establishing a legitimate government supported by the people and able to address the fundamental causes that insurgents use to gain support."[24] A U.S. Ambassador to Afghanistan during this time told the author that, in his view, "The overwhelming first requirement for governmental legitimacy is the provision of security. The provision of services is very much a secondary issue, and have historically had no relationship to legitimacy."[25]

By late summer 2008, the overall trend in RC-East was positive, and a functioning system of local governance was under construction. However, the government had not yet achieved legitimacy in many places, and was only beginning to develop the ability to address the conditions that allowed the insurgency to gain limited support. Local factors, such as tribal structures and the considerable capabilities of coalition forces, helped prevent insurgent forces from gaining a critical mass of support. While the presence of a Taliban shadow government in RC-East seemed minimal compared to some provinces in Regional Command-South (RC-South), gaps in coverage invited an insurgent presence.

A lack of trained civil servants was the greatest challenges to achieving adequate local governance. There was no quick fix to this, although establishing regional civil service academies and providing adequate pay put forward some hope. Corruption and the appearance of corruption were endemic in RC-East and was perhaps the second largest challenge. This was corrosive to COIN efforts and difficult to counter, given how culturally ingrained it was. The judicial system was struggling, and there appeared to be a lack of will at high levels of the government to confront corruption. On the positive side, RC-East had only limited narcotics trafficking (with the exception of Nangarhar in some years), which reduced the levels of corruption in comparison with RC-South, where the drug trade flourished. Increasing tax revenues to support government bureaucracies and fund services at the local level was also a challenge. Funds came from the central government and to some extent, local donors, but with the exception of some municipal taxes (and informal revenue), the local governments had no means to support themselves.

The security situation became markedly worse in the spring of 2005 as insurgent groups became more effective, preventing NGOs from having a large presence in border provinces. This not only restricted flows of funds, but also limited access for civilian experts on governance, and Coalition officers had to fill some of this gap. At the same time, the Coalition civilian component during this period was numerically inadequate. While many political officers were dedicated, competent, and effective, there were not enough of them, and as a result, the governance pillar did not move forward as much as it could have. At the same time, U.S. programs supporting local governments were not always coordinated with programs of the international community, and vice-versa, in part due to the limited presence of international donors in parts of –RC-East.

The growth of local government required the coalition to adjust its practices. While in 2004 the PRTs and battalions had to fill vacuums of governance in some areas, by 2008 Afghan officials were very much in the lead in many places, and the coalition had accordingly reduced its role.

As Afghan security forces increased their presence, local government became counterparts in security efforts, and in setting some policies that provided a framework for security efforts. The establishment of effective local government was also important to keep the Afghan military from being tempted to become involved in political affairs.

Provincial government was also an important testing ground for the next generation of Afghan national leadership, where leaders could gain experience and develop their political platforms.

Nangarhar governor Haji Din Muhammed (center) with USAID, State, and U.S. Military officials, Jalalabad, winter 2004.

Governor of Ghazni Province Khosti (center) along with Independent Electorate for Local Government officials and PRT officers.

U.S. ambassador Ronald Neumann and Khost governor Patan at an inauguration, 2005.

6

Development and Reconstruction

The large infusion of development funds into RC-East during the period 2004–2008 clearly supported COIN efforts at the tactical level. At a strategic level the correlation between COIN and projects was less clear. The option of spending heavily on development was an asymmetric advantage that the Taliban and other insurgent groups could not match. It also provided a degree of acceptance for an international presence among a more traditional and, at times, suspicious, population that was mostly Pashtun. Many of these development programs, including the military Commander's Emergency Response Program (CERP), showed some degree of success. However, various structural problems during this time hindered progress – including the lack of Afghan Government capacity, shortfalls USG interagency cooperation, the imbalance between civilian and military staff, the differing timelines between various players, and the inherent difficulty of rebuilding a very poor country in the middle of an insurgency that gained momentum during this period.

This chapter will examine a variety of issues. Did small, medium and large-scale projects carried out by USAID, through CERP, and to some extent the international community and the Afghan government enable a COIN campaign based on three main pillars: security, governance and economic development? How did the various organizations involved coordinate? How did the local Afghan population perceive these reconstruction and development efforts? Did these reconstruction and development projects reinforce and enable the security and governance pillars of the COIN strategy, while weakening the insurgency? What were the lessons learned?

These were contentious issues, that will continue to be debated for years.

Macroeconomic Factors

During this period the Afghan GDP grew quickly (in part due to the amount of international aid coming in), but how much this growth filtered down to rural and border areas in RC-East is debatable. Although many Afghans along the border used Pakistani rupees in addition to afghanis, the stable exchange rate of the Afghan currency was a positive factor, as were low inflation rates. Perhaps more important locally were the multiplier effects of cash from payroll and purchases for military bases, the benefits from the transit of NATO supplies (particularly through the Khyber Pass and into Nangarhar), the smuggling of goods brought duty free into Afghanistan—then smuggled back into Pakistan and remittances from overseas workers. While drug production did not reach the levels seen in RC-South, in some years Nangarhar had considerable poppy production, which would have injected significant amounts of money into the local economy.

GOA, AID, CERP, and Other Development Programs Relevant to COIN

GOA

During this period the Afghan Government at all levels – national, provincial, district and municipal – was undergoing a slow and difficult process of reestablishing itself. Rebuilding (or building) government in the middle of an insurgency, with limited human and financial resources, was difficult, and tribes and communities often provided governance where the reach of the formal government did not extend. At least on paper, Afghanistan had one of the world's most centralized governments, which put control of development planning and funding in the ministries in Kabul. At the same time, the ministries were "stovepiped," with lines of authority extending directly to officials of that ministry in the provinces, often bypassing governors' or mayors' offices, and making interagency coordination difficult. Several PRTs organized interagency meetings to improve coordination between ministry representatives at the provincial level.

The most active ministries in RC-East during this time were the Ministry of Agriculture, Irrigation and Livestock (MAIL); Ministry of Rural Rehabilitation and Development (MRRD); Ministry of Education; and Ministry of Public Health. Both the Ministry of Border and Tribal Affairs, and the Ministry of Women's Affairs were underfunded and understaffed, and the latter encountered some opposition in culturally conservative Pashtun areas. After its creation in 2007, the IDLG was increasingly active, and organized local government to formulate development plans, while also trying to expand its authority into spending development funds, including CERP. One of the more successful development schemes was the community-based National Solidarity Program, under the MRRD, and the Basic Package of Health Services, established in 2003 under the Ministry of Public Health.

At the national and international levels, the Interim-Afghanistan National Development Strategy (I-ANDS, and eventually, the ANDS and the Afghanistan Reconstruction Trust Fund) provided overarching frameworks. However, these plans were just beginning to be implemented, and local Afghan officials, as well as coalition officers were often not well-informed about them. A "lead nation" concept was agreed to at the Tokyo donor's conference in 2002. With this plan, individual nations took responsibility for a developmental sector. For example, Italy was to lead on justice, while the Germany took responsibility for the police. However, this concept did not translate to results on the ground in RC-East.

USAID
According to a report of the U.S. General Accounting Office (GAO) "In 2002 and 2003, USAID initially focused on humanitarian and short-term assistance, such as assistance to displaced persons and food assistance."[26] "In 2004, USAID expanded assistance to include quick impact projects, such as infrastructure projects." By the end of the period, USAID was following an integrated strategy—intended to "create economic growth, effective and representative governance, and the human capital base needed to eliminate the conditions that breed extremism."[27] Programs included road construction and rehabilitation (including farm-to-market roads), development of electrical networks, credit and microcredit programs,

and assistance in the privatization of state-owned enterprises. There was also an agricultural component—including irrigation and alternative livelihoods (aimed at diminishing poppy cultivation)—governance, health, as well as a large education program. AID was providing considerable funds to Afghanistan; a 2008 AID report noted that "With over $3.4 billion spent on development programs in Afghanistan since 2002, USAID provides the largest bilateral civilian assistance program to Afghanistan."[28]

In RC-East during this period, most AID field personnel were based out of PRTs, with some posted to brigade commands. Many were contractors on one-year assignments. At the same time, AID was awarding large-scale contracts for development projects to contractors such as the International Organization for Migration (IOM) and Development Alternatives Inc. (DAI). As a Senate report notes, "From FY 2007 to FY 2009, USAID obligated about $3.8 billion to 283 contractors and other entities," and that "Two contractors—Louis Berger International and Development Alternatives Inc.—accounted for about $1 billion [29] AID officers in RC-East often faced hurdles in monitoring the contracts, due to security challenges and lack of transportation. At the same time, contracting organizations (including the IOM) were slow to carry out some contracts due to security concerns.

CERP

As noted in the CERP Handbook produced by the Center for Army Lessons Learned, "CERP funds provide tactical commanders a means to conduct multiple stability tasks that have traditionally been performed by U.S., foreign, or indigenous professional civilian personnel or agencies. These tasks include but are not limited to the reconstruction of infrastructure, support to governance, restoration of public services, and support to economic development."[30] CERP funds could also be used for repairs due to combat damage, and condolence payments.

In RC-East during this period, the PRTs were the primary conduits of CERP funds, although maneuver battalions and, in some instances, brigade commands used them as well. The greatest advantage of CERP funds was the flexibility and speed with which they could be used (in contrast to many USAID projects, which were subject to significantly more mandatory oversight and reviews). This allowed the PRTs to provide funding for projects immediately after combat operations, and also quickly seize opportunities where communities or tribes were open to aligning themselves with Coalition forces and the Afghan government.

During the earlier years of this period, most CERP projects were relatively small, including building or refurbishing of schools, health clinics, markets, irrigation systems, and the upgrading of existing roads. By 2007, large amounts of funding were being channeled through CERP, with some PRTs handling tens of millions of dollars—a major shift in COIN efforts. The GAO noted in one report, "Since 2004, DOD has reported total obligations of about $1 billion for CERP in Afghanistan, growing from $40 million in FY 2004 to $486 million in FY2008. As of April 2009, Congress allocated… $683 million to fund CERP projects in Afghanistan.[31] While some of these CERP funds also went to other RCs, it clearly altered the military's role in –RC-East, from doing more "tactical" projects to being a major development player. For example, major road projects were begun through mountainous areas in Konar and Nuristan that required long timelines and considerable engineering.

While this increased funding made a positive impact in many places (particularly some road projects) it also strained the capacity of the civil affairs units and PRTs in terms of engineering, quality assurance/quality control (QAQC), and planning, despite the best efforts of those on the ground. The GAO report notes: "The (CERP) program has evolved over time in terms of the cost and complexity of projects…" and "In a July 2008 memorandum to CENTCOM [U.S. Central Command], the CJTF [Combined Joint Task Force] commanding general noted that, in some provinces, units have repositioned or are unable to do quality-assurance and quality-control checks due to competing missions and security risks."[32]

Particularly after the expansion of its budgets in 2007 and afterwards, the augmented CERP program pushed the military into areas that many view as falling in the domain of AID, international donors, and NGOs. To some extent, this was intentional – military officers, from captains to generals, remarked to the author that more traditional development programs were moving too slowly to support the military's COIN strategy and tactics, or were not present in areas the military considered as priorities. As one U.S. Army officer noted: : "While the U.S. Army is uniquely trained, manned, and equipped to operate in unstable regions, it lacks the development capacity and expertise of its civilian partners in conducting these tasks. However, civilian diplomatic and development agencies are often challenged to address such tasks in unstable areas with their traditional delivery systems."[33]

Agricultural Development
Much of the population of RC-East, which included practically everyone in rural areas, was involved in agriculture in one form or another. This fact made it necessary to focus on agriculture, especially given the more rural nature of the insurgency in some areas. Improvement and reconstruction of irrigation systems, as well as farm-to-market roads, were early efforts. However, U.S. Department of Agriculture (USDA) officers were present only in some PRTs, and then had very limited (if any) funding at their disposal. Beginning in 2008, the U.S. military began deploying "Agribusiness Development Teams" (ADTs), National Guard units whose soldiers brought agricultural, animal husbandry, and agribusiness skills. The first ADT deployed to Nangarhar in 2008, followed by a Texas unit in Ghazni.

Education
Education is a key to the democratic future of Afghanistan—it will be difficult to maintain a viable democracy without it. At the same time, a more educated workforce will be needed to form a civil service cadre to govern the country, to provide a workforce for businesses, and to counter the Taliban's propaganda aimed against the Afghan government and coalition forces. Hence, this is an important COIN aspect as well. During the early years of the 2004-2008 period, the Ministry of Education was still extending its reach into parts of RC-East, and suffered from scarce resources, including teachers. While the PRTs built schools, the Ministry did not necessarily have the means to use them, and teacher salaries were very low. Education in *madrassas* (educational institutions, either secular or religious), both locally and across the border in Pakistan, was an option that many parents took. In conversations with the author

and in surveys, Afghan parents put a priority on education for their children (including daughters in many cases).

USAID invested heavily in education across Afghanistan. By 2011, their programs had printed more than 97 million textbooks for grades 1 through 12, trained more than 53,000 teachers (including radio-based teacher training), and built or refurbished 680 schools. AID also supported programs for adult literacy and vocational training.[34] NATO numbers further suggest very strong improvements in RC-East. Although there is still much to be done, education seems to have been a bright spot among development efforts. The World Bank notes that by 2011, across Afghanistan 6.2 million Afghan students were attending grades 1 through 12, of whom 2.2 million are females. However, the World Bank notes that there remains "an acute shortage of teachers – many teachers do not receive their salaries on time, and have little or no training."[35] At the same time, schools were easy targets for insurgent attacks in some areas.

Other USG Programs

The Performance-Based Governor's Fund, intended to provide governors with administrative funds to run their offices and maintain a staff, through the transfer of roughly $25,000 per month, was put in place at the end of this period. According to the IDLG, (which oversaw the program, although it was administered by the Asia Foundation) it was intended "to provide interim financial assistance to Governors so they are better able to meet operational and community outreach needs, enhance their relationships with citizens and improve their overall management capacity."[36]

The State Department's Bureau for International Narcotics and Law Enforcement Affairs (INL) had its own "Good Performers Initiative" (GPI), launched in 2007, to reward provinces that eliminated or sharply reduced (by 10% or more) their poppy cultivation. This money was granted for development projects, in coordination with the governors and provincial development councils. Both of these programs were much smaller than the CERP and AID programs, but held considerable potential to improve provincial governance and development programs by tailoring programs to local conditions to attain specific policy goals.

Cooperation between Development Actors

Coordination between the various development and reconstruction players in RC-East during this period was, unsurprisingly, a major challenge. Different goals, organizational cultures, the inherent difficulties of operating in a country as unstable as Afghanistan, rapid turnover of foreign staff, and the need to adhere to guidelines passed down from Washington (or Kabul, Brussels or New York) made this hard. Interestingly, personalities and personal connections often made the difference, allowing obstacles to be overcome.

Coordination between development actors during the earlier years of this period was often ad-hoc, with field officers working together to try to resolve program conflicts at their level. Within the USG in 2004, the challenge of forming an overall, interagency strategy, coupled with insufficient information exchanges and considerable differences between the USAID, State, and Army bureaucracies led to coordination challenges in RC-East. Other players in the USG included the embassy-based Afghanistan Reconstruction Group (ARG) charged with advising embassy and Afghan officials on commercial and economic policy and attracting corporations to Afghanistan.

By 2008, USG efforts were more efficient and logical. The Integrated Civil-Military Action Group (ICMAG), established in 2008 within the U.S. embassy, pulled together senior State, AID, and military officers with roles in development for regular meetings, and fed into a higher-level Executive Working Group. State's S/CRS (the Office of the Coordinator for Reconstruction and Stabilization) provided officers to do interagency planning at both the embassy, brigade and PRT levels. Brigade commands served as the nexus in the field for coordinating projects across several provinces, and PRTs did the same for individual provinces. Nangarhar Inc., described elsewhere, brought together USG players involved in COIN, counternarcotics and long-term development.[37]

Towards the end of this period, the Afghan government at the national and, in some cases, provincial levels had begun to take a more active role in development coordination; by 2007 Provincial Development Plans (PDPs) had been produced for all provinces. At a higher level, the GOA and UN chaired the Joint Coordination Monitoring Board (established in 2006), to implement the Afghanistan Compact (agreed in 2006), including development activities under the I-ANDS.

Some Challenges to Development as a COIN Pillar

During this period there were considerable challenges to reconstruction and development programs. The possibility of attacks by insurgents after the Taliban and other groups began to extend their operations in the spring of 2005 restricted (or in some cases completely stopped) efforts by various development players. It also added considerable overhead to pay for security, and made the actual implementation of projects that much harder. The lack of Afghan capacity, in terms of trained development workers and government officials, slowed efforts. Rapid turnover of officers— military, State, AID (or UNAMA) often deployed on 12-month tours— led to a lack of continuity. Corruption on the part of GOA officials, or the perception of endemic corruption by Afghan citizens, hindered project implementation and their public relations benefits.

There was considerable debate—and acrimony—over the "humanitarian space," roughly defined as the provision of emergency relief, development and reconstruction assistance to the civilian population. Many NGOs believed, by virtue of experience, neutrality, and mandate, that they should set the terms and strategies for development assistance in these areas. At the same time, the lack of civilian security prevented NGOs from operating in many parts of RC-East during this time. Inevitably, this led to tensions with the military, as they filled what they perceived as a gap in development work that was an important pillar of their strategy (and despite the fact that the military often did not want the role). While UNAMA theoretically could help resolve problems and coordinate among players, in practice its limited numbers on the ground— and general lack of funding—reduced its influence. In the field, UNAMA could suggest, but not dictate.

The "metrics" of development and reconstruction projects— quantifying the number of projects underway or completed—was somewhat straightforward for the military, which had in place systems to collect and present this information. Metrics became more complex, however, when they were intended to assess the quality of projects—not only how well was the work done, but how much a project benefited the recipients, and how much it advanced coalition goals, including COIN. The difference in metrics between the military, USAID, and other donors—in terms of methodology and what goals were being evaluated—added another layer of complexity.

A related challenge was the incompatibility of databases; U.S. military was using its system, AID another, and the GOA was relying on a third. By 2008, an effort was launched within the U.S. embassy to resolve this issue, but merging separate databases was challenging. In some cases, there was not a central repository of data previously collected—it resided on hard drives, thumb drives and servers, of different units and officers who had long since departed Afghanistan. The mundane problem of different e-mail systems between State, AID, ISAF, the US military and the Afghan government made information sharing harder than it needed to be, as did the military's tendency to put much data on the classified Secret Internet Protocol Router Network (SIPRNet) system.

Quality assurance also presented challenges, particularly in areas with security problems. While the military could visit projects if convoys were available (dependent on military priorities), it was much more difficult for AID workers to move around—they often had to rely on military patrols that might or might not go to all the places they needed to visit. NGOs also tended to avoid moving with the military in order to maintain their status as neutral players. Long-term maintenance of projects was also a challenge; with very limited budgets, the Afghan government (particularly at the local level) did not necessarily have the means to maintain large projects such as roads.

Afghan Perceptions

What did the Afghans in RC-East think about these development efforts? The answer seemed to change over time. In 2004 the mood was one of hope, with the expectation that the international community would bring the resources and capabilities to improve people's lives. By 2008, the overall mood changed, as these expectations were often not met. One factor was that, while Afghans heard of large international donations arriving in Kabul, they often didn't see immediate returns and came to the conclusion the money was feeding corruption or funding comfortable lifestyles among foreign aid workers in Kabul. This depended on location; while rural areas remained poor, some towns such as Jalalabad, Khost, and Ghazni saw relative progress. Some districts received significant (by local standards) flows of money, and areas where large road projects emerged received direct benefits.

Did the assistance projects mesh with what Afghans wanted? In the author's experience, at the local level Afghans themselves were sometimes divided about what they wanted, with different parts of a community or different tribes having different priorities. Considerable effort was put into prioritizing projects, with coalition officers doing numerous, sometimes repetitive, surveys. These were often coupled with shura sessions, which allowed a community to debate and (sometimes) concur on proposed projects. Some requests, such as grid electricity, were difficult to provide over a short or medium time-frame, while basic services— health and education were a priority in most areas— required time to build up a functioning system.

Particularly along the insecure border areas with Pakistan, and increasingly after the insurgency gained momentum in 2005 momentum in 2005, security was the priority for many Afghans. Beyond that, many Afghans in RC-East, especially in rural areas, live at a subsistence level. As a result, jobs that augmented income from small-scale farming were the priority. This was a critical COIN issue as well—offering young men more than insurgent groups might pay to carry a gun or set off IEDs was a strong rationale for creating jobs. A national survey by the Asia Foundation published in 2008 notes that, after security issues, the most important were "economic issues including unemployment (31%), high prices (22%), poor economy (17%), and corruption (14%). This study also notes that "The most important local problems relate to lack of basic infrastructure such as electricity (30%), water (22%), and roads (18%)", and that "at an aggregate national level, electricity supply is ranked as the top priority, followed by water supply, roads, health care, and education."[38]

Did Large Amounts of Money Contribute to COIN Efforts?

Although it is very difficult to quantify in any meaningful way, in the author's experience, development assistance in RC-East during the period 2004–2008 clearly contributed to improving the lives of many people in eastern Afghanistan and supported COIN efforts. In a broader sense, it increased tolerance of U.S. forces operating in an area traditionally hostile to outsiders, where the population weighed the direct benefits of U.S. assistance against any perceived need to force foreigners out. Projects in the earlier part of this period seemed to provide a sense of hope among a population that, after decades of war, was exhausted and probably suffering from a form of communal post-traumatic stress disorder. Among other programs, those sponsored by USAID contributed to the establishment of a sustainable economy in –RC-East, and CERP filled some short and medium term gaps. Importantly, these development programs provided something the insurgents couldn't match, and therefore gave COIN an "asymmetric" advantage. Some jobs programs probably held down poppy production by providing alternative livelihoods, which in turn helped prevent a large-scale narcotics problem that would have made COIN even more complex in RC-East.

Field officers and current studies come to a variety of conclusions regarding any positive correlation between development programs and effective COIN. Several U.S. military officers told the author that road projects under CERP clearly had positive COIN effects. The Afghans saw the roads as having direct practical benefits—by providing access to markets, as well as a source of construction employment—which the insurgents could not match. Roads also showed the provincial Afghan government was functioning and making a positive impact, while making it easier for government officials to reach the population, and for shuras to be organized in mountainous terrain. Completed road projects also showed that the international community got results, and was not just making plans and proposals. Similarly, CERP served the military in "economy of force" situations, where projects provided a presence and an impact in areas where patrols were infrequent due to limited numbers of soldiers. On the other hand, a State officer with responsibility for several border provinces told the author in

2011 that very few large development projects were achieving their goals.

David Kilcullen, in his excellent study of road building projects during this period in Konar, notes an additional benefit: the road building project "seems to be succeeding because people have used the process of the roads construction, especially the close engagement with district and tribal leaders this entails, as a framework around which to organize a full-spectrum strategy…to separate insurgents from the people, win local allies, connect the population to the government, build local governance capacity, modify and improve governance capacity, (and) swing tribes that had supported the insurgency into the government side."[39] Kilkullen is positive about the COIN effects, noting a "conscious and well-developed strategy that uses the road as a tool, and seizes the opportunity to generate security, economic, governance and political benefits."[40] A common saying among military officers at this time was that "security ends where the road ends," underscoring the importance of these projects for security forces as well.

Malkasian and Meyerle make a positive connection between development projects and COIN effects during research carried out in –RC-East during 2007 and 2008. They note that "in Khost an aggressive project 'blitz' corresponded with fewer attacks and the emergence of a real partnership between tribes and the government. In Konar, road projects in two major river valleys led to a rise in local community political participation and local resistance to insurgent activity. In Ghazni, PRT projects appear to have helped counter rising violence, and the PRTs focus on reducing corruption and improving Afghan public health can be said to have improved governance."[41]

However, a 2010 Wilton Park conference that brought together military, government officials, and development workers to examine the effectiveness of development on COIN in Afghanistan came to some less positive conclusions.[42] Among other views, the conference concluded that when development assistance often provided stabilization benefits at a tactical level, the longer-term strategic benefits were less clear. The conference also noted that "Too much aid money spent quickly with little oversight can be delegitimizing and destabilizing in many ways, including by: fuelling corruption;

creating destabilizing winner-loser dynamics in ethnically and tribally divided societies; supporting a lucrative war/aid economy that benefits insurgents, corrupt government officials, and other malign actors; and creating perverse incentives among key actors to maintain the status quo of insecurity and bad governance."

Andrew Wilder in his perceptive 2009 paper makes a similar argument, saying "...despite counterinsurgency doctrine's heavy reliance on the assumption that aid 'wins hearts and minds' not to mention the billions of dollars being spent on it, there is remarkably limited evidence from Afghanistan supporting a link between aid and stability." Wilder makes the case that "As the conflict has proceeded, Afghans' perceptions of U.S. and international aid, as well as those who deliver it (be they military forces, the government, aid contractors, or NGOs) have grown overwhelmingly negative." [43]

Perhaps the best conclusion at this time is that development projects clearly provided tactical benefits for COIN. Strategic gains may well be mixed, but it will take years for this to be clear. Separately, the infusion of large amounts of assistance funding almost certainly fueled corruption, and there is a danger of establishing a culture of dependency on foreign assistance as well. It is also worth considering how much these projects will benefit the Afghan government and security forces in the future, as U.S. forces draw down and hand off difficult provinces such as Konar. Will the clear COIN benefits from the construction of roads remain after the eventual handoff to the Afghan government, or will entirely new projects be needed to maintain any counterinsurgency momentum?

Development Lessons Learned

The large infusion of development funds into RC-East supported COIN efforts, provided an asymmetrical advantage—projects that improved people's lives, and improves prospects for their children's future—that the Taliban and other insurgent groups could not match. It also provided "space" and a degree of acceptance for an international presence among a traditional, at times suspicious population that was mostly Pashtun. Otherwise, the local population would most likely have met this presence—particularly a military presence— with considerably more hostility, given the experiences of previous foreign militaries.

Given the very low standard of living, particularly in rural areas, small and less expensive projects could often make a positive impact on people's lives in the short term. For example, improvements to existing irrigation systems, community projects to pave roads with stones, improvement of market areas, refurbishment or construction of school buildings, or assistance with crop or livestock production often had a very good cost/benefit ratio. While nascent during this period, microcredit schemes had considerable potential.

Many different "clocks" were in play on development issues during this period, coupled with differing cultures. The U.S. military wanted (and at times was able) to move quickly, and get results. This reflected a "can-do" culture, tours of less than 15 months (which spurred officers to get projects accomplished in this time frame), and the reality that development was a key to COIN—and to saving soldiers' lives. USAID was often more deliberate, using years of experience in what works best in development—while at the same time being more restrained by regulations and oversight relative to CERP. Big international donors such as the Asian Development Bank moved slowly, in part due to the size of their programs. Afghan society, particularly in rural areas, often moved to the slow rhythm of an agricultural, consensus-based society. These three very different speeds led to inevitable, and considerable friction, which was not always managed well and hindered coordination. While not a development player (except perhaps in the justice sector, where they delivered a rough form of justice in some areas), the Taliban and other insurgent groups had yet another "clock"— the perception that from their sanctuaries in Pakistan, they could outwait the international community.

During the early part of the period 2004–8, much of the development was still ad-hoc, and lacking in overall strategy or goals. By 2008, various larger-scale programs were in place. Also, GOA development strategies were not yet being presented or implemented systematically. There were disconnects at times between coalition efforts and the national framework, or large-scale international schemes, in part due to a lack of communications. The framework of the newly developed ANDS, for example, was not necessarily used as a guideline, and commanders managing large

CERP accounts were not always aware of Asian Development Bank and EU projects (to pick two examples) that were planned for or underway in their areas of operation.

There was the perception during this period, voiced most strongly by governors but also by some in the central government, that provinces with security challenges - particularly an active insurgency - received more assistance than relatively stable areas. Some governors believed that efforts to limit insurgency in their provinces had the unintended result of reduced attention and assistance from the international community.

By 2007 PRTs were receiving increased CERP funding relative to previous years, in some cases tens of millions of dollars. While each PRT had different capacities, at times this stretched their abilities to identify the best potential projects, carry out project design, get buy-in from the involved communities, and carry out project oversight. This funding surge may have also reduced PRTs' ability to do other tasks, as development crowded out political or public relations work, to name two examples. Also, while the need for development projects in local communities seemed inexhaustible due to low initial baselines, there may have been limits in the ability to absorb aid in relatively short time spans.

Afghan society is complex at all levels—national, provincial, and local—and this complexity had a direct impact on development projects. A detailed knowledge of the local dynamics was crucial to planning and implementing successful projects. This was never simple, and presented coalition officers with the continual possibility of making mistakes. For example, rivalries between tribes or communities often went back decades, and lack of awareness of this could result in officers inadvertently backing one group over another through project planning and implementation—possibly leading to anti-coalition feelings, and/or failed projects. A related complication were the risks communities and their leaders sometimes ran in accepting projects – insurgents at times targeted those who cooperated with counter-insurgents or the Afghan government.

A related issue during the period 2004–2008 was the rapid rotation of units and officers through Afghanistan. Later in the decade the USG made an effort to improve the transfer of local

Development and Reconstruction 63

and regional knowledge, and rotate the same military units and civilians, through the same area, both of which showed positive results.

Perhaps an even more fundamental issue during this period was the imbalance of civilian to military personnel on the ground in RC-East. With each PRT often having only two or three civilians from State, AID, and USDA (and often less in 2004-2005), and similar numbers in brigade commands, there were simply not enough civilians to manage development issues, and military officers therefore were pressed into service in these areas. While the military did have civil-military affairs units on the ground, they were themselves insufficient to cover the range of activities and the increasing flows of CERP funds by 2007, so that military officers in other specialties at times covered development issues.

Development projects and programs during this period, particularly CERP, seemed strongly oriented towards infrastructure, with less emphasis on the development of human resources and government institutions. In particular, the development of a larger, more adept civil service cadre was lacking. The lack of progress in building civil institutions relative to some of the security-related institutions was a weakness in the COIN strategy. The rapid rotation of military and civilian officers may have been a factor, in that building a civil service cadre in Afghanistan will require extended effort over many years—and is not something that can be achieved over a short tour.

The gradual reduction in USAID Foreign Service officers over years and decades had a direct impact on operations along the border, as AID either had to rely more on short-term contractors or had to endure staffing gaps. Compared with the number of career officers and programs deployed during the war in Vietnam, where they deployed large numbers of career officers to the field, AID's resources were badly stretched during this war. Concurrently, a lack of multiyear funding was a structural problem with major implications for COIN.

The sustainability of projects—such as the maintenance of roads - presented serious long-term challenges in Afghanistan. While smaller, low-tech projects that had community buy-in could succeed without much GOA support, more complex projects—

especially those that require a steady stream of maintenance funds and technological/engineering capabilities—were challenging. The pressure to get projects completed during relatively short rotations almost certainly hindered sustainability, as the number of projects completed took precedence over putting in place the means to sustain them.

As CERP evolved in Afghanistan, one of its greatest advantages was the devolution of decision making to lower levels. Although oversight was in place for review of project packets by the military chain of command, considerable responsibility was given to lieutenants, captains and majors in the field. These officers often had the best visibility into the needs of communities, and which projects might have the greatest COIN payoffs.

Afghanistan is subject to various natural disasters, including earthquakes, floods and outbreaks of disease. USAID and the military were often able to provide disaster relief, thanks to logistical capabilities, experience, manpower, and ready funding. These efforts often built good will among the population. Similarly, band-aid efforts such as "medcaps" and "vetcaps" that delivered immediate medical or veterinary assistance to rural areas or villages often yielded local goodwill.

From a long-term perspective, the improvement in the educational system, in terms of quality, quantity, and access, will form the underpinnings of any sustainable democracy. This may be easier than it appears – Afghan parents seem to put a priority on learning.

Large-scale projects such as electricity generation and transmission, while fundamental to the economic development of RC-East, were clearly beyond the scope of PRTs and to some extent AID efforts in RC-East during this time. Fortunately, later projects, particularly those bringing electricity from Central Asia, may help resolve this fundamental challenge.

One long-term result of the amounts of money invested, the projects completed, (as well as the foreign military and civilian presence) is the partial transformation of Pashtun society. Roads that opened up previously isolated valleys, the improved education system, and the provision of electricity, among others, changed this part of the world. Commercially driven changes such as the rapid expansion of cell phone coverage have done the same. This rapid social transformation may have fueled some parts of the insurgency, as a violent reaction to modernization.

There has been a lively debate, both within governments and in the academic press, over how much international development funds have fueled corruption in the Afghan government, and by extension Afghan society. While this is difficult to quantify, it is hard not to conclude that the large amounts of money, coupled with at times loose oversight, weak legal structures, and a mentality among some Afghans that it is best to grab what is available now as insurance against future instability, have not caused more corruption. Similarly, there are concerns over how much dependency the massive aid flows, relative to Afghan GDP, are causing. Again, it is hard to escape the conclusion that, given GOA fiscal realities and cultural tendencies, some degree of dependency has been formed.

Microeconomics—in the sense of jobs, affordable necessities such as food, and household standard of living—were critical to long-term success of COIN efforts. If people saw their living standards increasing (or at least not getting worse) this led to more support for the government, and more acceptance of a foreign presence.

As a basic tenant of development, mechanisms to hand the maintenance of projects over to the Afghans—government, NGOs and communities—was of fundamental importance. In the rush to get projects moving in the early part of this period, this sort of planning was not always a priority. In a related issue, community "ownership" of projects was not always optimal. Infrastructure, such as schools or medical clinics, did not fully benefit communities if Afghan staff and administrative support was not yet in place. The centralization of the Afghan state also presented challenges to local ownership of projects, as did the difficulty of doing regional projects that involved multiple provincial governments, who were not accustomed, or organized, to work together. Importantly, expectation management by the international community was difficult—many Afghans expected more than the international community could deliver, while at times too many promises were made.

Epilogue: U.S. Development Efforts after 2008

Many of the impediments to efficient development work in RC-East during the period of 2004–2008 have since received high-level attention within the USG, with various positive results. As a 2011 Senate staff report concludes: "The U.S. effort [in Afghanistan] began in earnest in 2009, when the administration and Congress recognized the need for properly resourcing the civilian effort."[44] The establishment within the State Department of the office of the Special Representative for Afghanistan and Pakistan (S/SRAP) under Ambassador Richard Holbrooke provided a single office where officers from various bureaus and agencies could exchange information and coordinate efforts. Amb. Holbrooke also headed a "civilian surge" that brought hundreds of additional officers into Afghanistan, both in the embassy and in field positions. He also pushed for improved coordination of development efforts along the Afghanistan-Pakistan border, and saw the need for more assistance in agriculture, recognizing how fundamental this is given the large number of Afghans who make a living through crops and livestock. The USG overall review of the Afghanistan strategy, carried out during the last months of 2009, also provided more direction to the overall effort. At the same time, the Afghan government has gradually increased its development capacity, as ministries expanded their staffing, put in place internal controls so that more funds could be provided directly to ministries for projects, and gained experience in project management and interagency coordination. Within the U.S. embassy in Kabul, new positions were created to improve development efforts, including an ambassador-level development coordinator (the Coordinating Director for Development and Economic Affairs). An RC-East civilian coordinator position was established in Bagram, and filled by a senior civil service officer, while civilian staffing at PRTs and brigade commands were significantly increased. More staffing was provided at the district level, and supported by programs such as the District Delivery Program, with AID funds reoriented to support projects and local governance at this level, particularly in "key terrain districts." In 2010, AID launched the "Accountable Assistance for Afghanistan" program to increase controls over its funding. During the same year, the U.S. military published a "Counterinsurgency Contracting Guidance" and established Task Force 2010 to address issues with contracting, so that "coalition forces have been doing a much better job of channeling assistance and construction dollars into the right hands."[45] NATO allies, particularly the Poles in Ghazni and the French in Kapisa, provided significant numbers of troops, while Turkey and the Czech Republic became involved in civilian efforts through their PRTs in Wardak and Logar Provinces, respectively.

Given the long border with Pakistan, and the difficulty of controlling the flow of people and contraband across it, what happens in Pakistan has considerable influence in the Afghan border provinces. The establishment of "border coordinators" at the U.S. embassies in Kabul and Islamabad was in part intended to coordinate development efforts, which was at times lacking in previous years. The decision to provide several billion dollars of additional assistance to Pakistan could also benefit border areas of Afghanistan. Importantly, the counterinsurgency efforts of the Pakistani military, particularly offensives in Swat, Mohmand, Bajaur, and South Waziristan—all of which border Afghanistan—could improve security enough that development efforts in Afghanistan are more effective (although by 2012 this did not appear to be the case).

During the period 2004–2008, the USG deployed to RC-East a cadre of talented, dedicated military and civilian officers, who made a considerable positive impact, despite risks and hardships. Given how damaged and underdeveloped much of this area was in 2001, the difficulty of reconstructing a nation in the middle of an active insurgency, and the challenges of getting programs and projects "right," the international community will need to be involved in Afghanistan for years, and probably decades, more.

7

Security

Improving security, expanding the reach of the Afghan National Security Forces (ANSF), and countering insurgents was the main effort in RC-East during this period, and considerable amounts of effort and money were expended towards this end. U.S. counterinsurgency and counterterrorism efforts in eastern Afghanistan in 2004 and 2005 were predominantly focused on the border with Pakistan, where the majority of combat operations took place. The provinces with the most active insurgencies were Khost, Paktia, Paktika and Konar Provinces, with security generally better away from the border and in non-Pashtun areas, such as Bamian and Panjshir Provinces. By 2008 this had changed considerably, with more fighting in parts of Ghazni, Wardak, and Logar Provinces.

Military writers and other authors have written excellent descriptions of military operations during this period.[46] This chapter provides context and gives the author's observations, but is not intended as an in-depth analysis of security operations during this time.

Most of the fighting during this period involved small units of insurgents, and sporadically intense firefights. The insurgents for the most part avoided moving and attacking in large units, which Coalition forces could fix and target with considerable firepower, either from ground forces, close-air support, artillery, or a combination of these. Attacks on larger bases failed, for similar reasons coupled with good perimeter security, although some assaults on smaller bases came closer to success for the insurgents, particularly in Konar and Nuristan. Seen from the level of brigade commands, RC-East had an almost constant stream of small unit "troops in contact" (TICs), IEDs, indirect fires of rockets and mortars, and small ambushes. Much of this had the feel of cat and mouse, rather than actions resulting in long-term strategic gains. This activity was seasonal—during the winter months it tapered off sharply, particularly in areas with heavy snowfall and cold weather. Big sweeps by battalion-sized forces often seemed to have limited results, in part because the insurgents went to ground—slipping into Pakistan, becoming farmers again, or hiding out. Population security in the larger towns such as Khost, Ghazni or Jalalabad was surprisingly good – there was only limited urban fighting, and not that many bombings during this time, compared to what could have been. Population security in rural areas along the border was difficult to achieve, however, due to the dispersed population in these areas.

In the end, the capacity and resilience of the ANSF is what will matter. The ANA made considerable gains in terms of capacity and development, and many of its officers and soldiers showed a real ability for small-unit operations—unsurprisingly, given Afghan history and culture. Operating in larger units, planning and logistical support were challenging for the ANA, but steady progress was made, overall.

U.S. Military Units

The U.S. and international military chains of command were complex during this time, and underwent several major changes in structure and leadership. There were separate, parallel chains, including the U.S. OEF; U.S. Special Forces and the Combined Joint Special Operations Task Force (CJSOTF); ISAF, which reported to NATO; and Combined Security Transition Command-Afghanistan (CSTC-A), charged with training Afghan security forces. In 2008, OEF was made subordinate to ISAF under the (U.S.) commander of ISAF Gen. McKiernan, in order to establish unity of command.

Combined Forces Command-Afghanistan (CFC-A) was established in November 2003 as the Coalition headquarters for Afghanistan, and reported to CENTCOM. CFC – A was commanded by a three-star general during this period, first by Lieutenant General (LTG) David Barno, followed by LTG Karl Eikenberry. The desired end-state of CFC-A was: "A moderate, stable and representative Afghanistan capable of controlling and governing its territory."[47] Subordinate to CFC-A was a series of Combined Joint Task Forces at the corps or division level, based out of Bagram, under which RC-East was subordinate. In October 2006 RC-East was nominally moved under ISAF command, at that time commanded by UK Gen. Richardson. In practice, this reorganization had limited impact at the field level; RC-East remained a U.S. show, and most enlisted troops had only the murkiest idea what their ISAF shoulder patches meant.

Brigade Commands

The brigade command in RC-East was central to the coordination of military efforts; development funding under CERP; some political activities; and training, mentoring, and joint operations with ANSF. Brigade commands also played an important role in interagency coordination with State, AID, and USDA; and liaison with other parts of the USG. They were also the main link to the CJTF in Bagram, and were key in coordination with Pakistani forces along the border. The brigade command oversaw PRT and maneuver battalion activities in RC-East, determining priorities, assigning resources and assessing progress. The following section will look at case studies of how two brigade commands carried out their job, from a civilian perspective.

Case Study: Combined Task Force (CTF) Devil

In 2005 the brigade command for RC-East was located in Khost at Forward Operating Base (FOB) Salerno, at that time the 1st Brigade of the 82nd Airborne. This command was subordinate to CJTF-76, at Bagram, and was known as "CTF Devil." The brigade was commanded by a full colonel, supported by a complete staff and augmented with liaison officers from subordinate and Special Forces units. The Deputy Commander, a lieutenant colonel, had overall responsibility for the PRTs. The brigade controlled eight PRTs (Asadabad, Jalalabad, Methar Lam, Gardez, Ghazni, Bamian, Khost, Sharan) and a complement of between four and five maneuver battalions, including marine and airborne units, for a total of roughly

5,000 personnel.

The strategy of CTF Devil for RC-East was nested within the larger OEF strategy and included:

- Conduct stability operations to defeat insurgents and separate them from the people.
- Protect the people in RC-East and interdict infiltrators from Pakistan's Federally Administered Tribal Areas (FATA).
- Transform the environment by building the Afghans' capacity to secure and govern themselves.[48]

CTF Devil correctly identified the Afghan population as the key: "The CTF's decisive operations would focus on the people, the center of gravity. For operations to succeed, coalition forces realized the people needed to believe they were secure. The task force found itself in competition with the Taliban for the will of the people."[49]

The U.S. military later added a second brigade combat team to the border areas of RC-East, including a second task force (TF)—TF Spartan— headquartered in Jalalabad. This brigade headquarters had responsibility for four provinces: Nangarhar, Konar, Laghman, and Nuristan (known as N2KL). This considerably increased the ability to carry out combat operations in areas that were previously "economy of force" operations—those with only a minimal presence, in order to allow a greater presence elsewhere—as well as increased partnering with ANA, Afghan Border Police (ABP) and Afghan National Police (ANP) units. It also had increased the level of security sufficiently that the PRTs could operate in districts where their movements had previously been restricted.

Case Study: Task Force Bayonet

In 2007 the 173rd Airborne Brigade Combat Team (ABCT) took over N2KL as "TF Bayonet", filling in behind the 3rd brigade, 10th Mountain "TF Spartan," headquartered at Jalalabad Air Field (JAF) just east of the city of Jalalabad. The 173rd had originally been designated to go to Iraq, and was already training for that deployment when it was redirected to Afghanistan. TF Spartan had aggressively expanded the joint US/Afghan presence in their area of operations, establishing numerous FOBs and combat outposts (COPs) The 173rd largely fell in on the strategy laid out by TF Spartan—perhaps, in part, because they were diverted from being deployed to Iraq to instead deploying to Afghanistan, on very short notice.

Beyond inheriting more than twenty-five FOBs and the smaller, less permanent COPs, TF Bayonet engaged in a very broad spectrum of activities. As with TF Devil, it coordinated the activities of PRTs in Jalalabad, Asadabad, Mehtar Lam and Nuristan; directed the operations of six battalions, and managed more than $100 million of CERP funds, which included amounts for extensive road and bridge construction projects. The TF also worked with the ANA, doing joint operations, training, and mentoring; focused on border control, including coordination with Pakistani security forces; had a substantial information operations program; and carried out a limited political program with Afghan officials.

TF Bayonet had some outstanding battalion and troop commanders, who adapted to some very complex situations and led well in difficult circumstances. Each of the four N2KL provinces presented very different challenges and opportunities, and the PRTs and battalions adjusted accordingly. For example, TF Saber, a cavalry troop based in Naray, adopted a population-centric approach that took into consideration a complex political and social situation. TF Rock, an airborne battalion, mixed hard combat operations with "softer" political and development efforts, an approach appropriate to their Konar area of operations (AO). The objectives of this task force included "separating insurgents from the population; stabilizing the AO; and transforming the area of operations for economic revitalization."[50] A list of duties (aside from combat operations) outlined by the battalion commander included running tactical operations centers and command posts; mentoring Afghan security forces; administering detention facilities; managing intelligence fusion centers; implementing CERP programs, and providing force protection for U.S. forces and parts of the Afghan government.[51]

Later in the deployment the TF was augmented by a helicopter detachment, considerably increasing its ability to carry out combat operations, defend firebases, and attack insurgent movements. This TF faced some heavy fighting, particularly in the Pesh Valley, the

Korangal Valley, and parts of Nuristan. As noted in the development chapter, this TF was an important player in integrated counter narcotics (CN) and development projects, including Nangarhar Inc.

This ambitious range of activities was a challenge to manage, even though the 173rd had a full colonel deputy commander who handled CERP and a range of other administrative issues, as well as very competent majors and lieutenant colonels on the brigade staff. Initially there were no civilians on the brigade staff, although the State Department filled a political advisor position in the fall of 2007 (the author), and AID and USDA provided officers by 2008. As a short-term fix for the lack of civilians, State's S/CRS detailed officers to TF Bayonet for part of 2008. Clearly, more civilian presence and expertise from the beginning of this TF deployment was needed.

By the time TF Bayonet rotated out in the summer of 2008, handing over to the 3rd Brigade Combat Team (BCT), 1st Infantry Division, "TF Duke," it had accomplished a great deal. Nangarhar had been largely stabilized, the Afghan government and security forces were in the lead, and the economy was fairly strong. Laghman Province showed steady progress in government and security. Konar and Nuristan were improving, although both of these provinces had such fundamental challenges—high mountains with harsh winters, several active insurgencies, weak infrastructure and governance, a history of fighting against outsiders, a long border with Pakistan, and limited economic potential—that only so much progress could be expected over a single (or multiple) deployments.

TF Bayonet achieved some fundamental and important goals. Security operations helped give the GOA and ANSF time to expand their reach, and the Coalition presence gave confidence to many Afghans. Aside from some more remote areas, the insurgents had limited success in holding territory, and did not threaten urban areas. The highway from the Khyber Pass through Nangarhar and Laghman, a critical supply route, was never closed during this period, and government organization at Torkham Gate improved. The Coalition presence in N2KL almost certainly shielded Kabul from attack. Among other development efforts, major road programs were carried out, opening up previously isolated areas.

In the months and years after the 173rd's deployment, there was considerable public debate over the tactic of dispersing more than twenty-five FOBs and COPs through the area of operations. While these smaller bases were more vulnerable to attack, and were often difficult to resupply, from a counterinsurgency perspective, this was the correct approach. They provided security for the local population, helped the ANA and GOA extend its reach, blocked insurgent resupply and transit routes, kept tabs on local conditions, and made it harder for insurgents to attack cities and towns. On the negative side, maintaining these bases required considerable commitment in terms of money, time and casualties, especially if it were to succeed in the longer term. Local conditions—a rising insurgency, operating both locally and out of sanctuaries, coupled with extremely rugged terrain—certainly made this an expensive proposition, as the Soviets found out in the 1980s when they conducted operations in Konar, and suffered considerable setbacks and casualties. An additional ten-to-fifteen-year commitment that controlling this part of Afghanistan would require with all the associated costs was almost certainly more than the Coalition was willing to support, but probably wasn't figured into the original calculations.

Another debate centered on the fight in the Korangal Valley, in Konar Province west of Asadabad. This was a protracted, low-intensity struggle in rugged conditions that resulted in considerable casualties (by Afghanistan standards) and the expenditure of considerable ordnance, by most standards. Part of the debate is a result of the complexity of the situation. The native Korangalis were insular; hostile to outside forces; culturally outliers; dedicated to protecting a timber/lumber industry that they felt was threatened, while hosting (either thorough coercion, or affiliation, or both) insurgent groups, including Arabs and other non-Afghans. Coalition and Afghan forces were trying to keep this rugged valley from becoming an insurgent base, and a staging area for attacks against population centers, including Kabul and Jalalabad. The conflict almost certainly took on a momentum of its own, with none of the various sides wanting to back down once the fight was joined.[52]

Maneuver Battalions

The tactics of each maneuver battalion in RC-East were considerably different, depending upon its internal capabilities, the training and equipment of the battalion, the guidance provided by the brigade command, the nature of the insurgency, the terrain, the capabilities of the local ANSF and GOA, informal Afghan security forces, and the personality and inclination of the battalion commander and his staff. This section looks at how these units operated in 2005, but this was not significantly different, overall, in later years.

In 2005 RC-East maneuver battalions were based in Orgun-E, Khost, Ghazni, and Jalalabad, and in most cases had more than one province in their AO. Each unit, comprising roughly 700 soldiers, was commanded by a lieutenant colonel, operating out of a Tactical Operations Center (TOC). These battalions were combat-oriented, constantly carrying out patrols, sweeps, cordon-and-search operations and occasional full-scale assaults in coordination with air assets. They were sufficiently strong that the Taliban and other insurgent units could not prevail in any protracted engagement, or be able to field units above twenty or thirty fighters. These efforts helped to secure the "humanitarian space" as well, providing enough cover so that PRTs, and in some cases NGOs, were able to operate more effectively.

The battalions also carried out reconstruction projects using CERP funding. These projects were often targeted at populations in areas with active insurgencies, with the aim of demonstrating the benefits of supporting the GOA and the Coalition, or were used in areas immediately after combat operations. By mid-2005, some maneuver units were contributing to the security of major road-building projects, which would not have been possible otherwise. Battalion officers also contributed to political development; the commanders were often in close contact with governors and (politically influential) police chiefs, in some cases acting as de facto advisors. At the district levels, captains were the counterparts of sub-governors in some areas, acting as advisors and helping with funding and security.

U.S. Special Forces Units in 2005

In 2005 the U.S. Special Forces had Operational Detachments-B (ODBs) at Khost, Jalalabad, and Orgun-E, with Operational Detachments-A (ODAs) deployed in many different areas, including several FOBs. These units engaged in a variety of activities, including direct action, some foreign internal defense (working with Afghan forces), "psychological operations" and reconstruction efforts.[53] At times, these forces cooperated closely with battalion and PRT efforts, which complemented the limited manpower of the ODAs, while contributing knowledge of the local situation.

Afghan Security Forces

Afghan security forces included the ANA, the ANP, the ABP, and the National Directorate of Security (NDS), with the last possessing both intelligence and law-enforcement responsibilities. All of these forces were being developed, and varied widely in strength and quality between—and sometimes within—provinces. Subordinate to the ANP were the Highway Police (later disbanded). Of these forces, the ANA was overall the most effective, and the most respected by the populace. The ANP often lacked equipment, funding and morale; they were also perceived by much of the population as being corrupt in various degrees. The deployment of these forces was uneven; Jalalabad, by the fall of 2005, had a substantial ANA garrison, while other provinces—Nuristan, Daikundi, and much of Paktika—had few if any troops deployed. In general, relations between the Afghan forces and the PRTs and maneuver units were cooperative.

Informal Afghan Forces

In addition to the formal security forces, there were a variety of informal units that played a role during this period. In the Pashtun areas there was the tradition of *alberkai*, tribal militias raised to provide security for specific events or emergencies. These were called up for both the 2004 presidential and the 2005 parliamentary elections, and performed well at the local level. Several tribal and local strongmen still controlled their own informal militias, but by the end of 2005, these had mostly been disbanded. In some areas, existing militias were endorsed by the GOA and Coalition until the ANA could take over; an example where this worked well was the 25th Afghan Militia Force, a battalion-sized unit, based in Khost, that complemented U.S. forces until regular ANA units were deployed to Khost.

Pakistani Security Forces

In Pakistan, the paramilitary Frontier Corps was deployed along the border, and in some ways was the most important counterpart to U.S. and Afghan forces. It had headquarters in both Peshawar and Quetta, and a total strength of roughly 65,000 men. The Frontier Corps was normally under the MOI, with regular military officers leading battalion-level units. In the NWFP it had 14 local units, including the well-known Khyber Rifles. Other forces included the *kassadars* (tribal policemen), along with tribal units including *alberkai* and *lashkars* (militiamen). None of these units were particularly well trained or equipped during this period.

The Pakistani Army's 11th Corps was headquartered in Peshawar. Beginning in 2002, the Pakistani military was increasingly active in the FATA, carrying out sweeps against some insurgent groups, particularly those with foreign fighters, and providing security in border areas in support of the 2005 Afghan elections. The U.S. provided considerable assistance through its Foreign Military Funding (FMF) program, and through Coalition Support Funds.

Review of Afghan National Army troops, Laghman Province, 2005.

Afghan National Police training class, Nangarhar Province.

Military and civilian security officials attend change of command ceremony, Paktika Province, Spring 2005.

Security 81

Light weapons turned in as part of DDR program, Laghman Province, 2005.

Troops loading into helicopter for an air assault.

8

The Role of Provincial Reconstruction Teams

PRTs, civilian-military platforms designed to extend the reach of the government of Afghanistan as well as carry out other functions, were one of the key efforts in RC-East.[54] This chapter examines several aspects of PRTs: What role did they play in COIN efforts in this part of Afghanistan, and what did they do that may have been detrimental? How could these concepts apply to insurgencies outside of Afghanistan?

This chapter considers three aspects: (1) the utility of PRTs, focusing on governance, diplomatic efforts, and civilian-military coordination, with some observations on the strategic significance of these efforts—U.S. Army Field Manual (FM) 3-24, *Counterinsurgency*, is a point of reference; (2) the challenges the PRTs faced in RC-East; (3) an overall assessment of their success or failure, and lessons learned.

PRTs were part of a larger Coalition team operating in conjunction with battalions, brigades, and Special Forces units. While each of these units had its specific tasks, they often blended together. This discussion focuses on the political role of PRTs, rather than their military or development assistance efforts.

Utility of PRTs

From a political officer's perspective, the political utility of PRTs between 2004 and 2008 were in three main areas:

- Assistance in developing local governance
- Reporting, analysis, and diplomacy

- As a hub for coordination within the U.S. government, with the government of Afghanistan (GoA), and with international organizations

PRT Lead Nations in Regional Command East, 2008

Developing Local Governance

The COIN manual notes, "The primary objective of any COIN operation is to foster development of effective governance by a legitimate government.[55]

How did PRTs contribute to this line of operation? While most international civilian efforts sought to establish a functioning central government in Kabul immediately after the 2001 defeat of the Taliban, by 2004 more effort was put into establishing and developing provincial-level governance. There was a need not only to build up governance, but also to reestablish a functioning civil society. PRTs were central to military, State Department, and to some extent, USAID programs to improve governance.[56] By 2007, more emphasis could be put on improving district-level government, along with some programs to build up municipal governments. Initially, PRTs in RC-East worked in a fluid environment, with uneven Afghan government presence and considerable influence by informal power brokers, including tribal leaders, militia leaders, mullahs, and landowners. The insurgency was still in its nascent stages, so that civilian and military coalition officers had more opportunities to engage with Afghans. Many, perhaps most, Afghan civilians at this time were hopeful about the country's future and positive regarding Coalition efforts. Taking advantage of these circumstances, the PRTs worked with maneuver units to move provincial government forward by providing CERP and AID funds, as well as mobility and security to governors and other officials. They also provided advice and assisted with information campaigns and interagency coordination within the Afghan government.

Working in conjunction with other coalition units and UN teams, the PRTs contributed significantly to the 2004 and 2005 elections by assisting with logistical support, campaigns to explain elections to the population (and to the candidates), and organizing security efforts. Team members also served as election observers. While far from perfect, these elections were important in putting at least some elected officials in place; the 2004 and 2005 elections, in particular, were seen as credible by many Afghans. However, by 2005 several insurgencies were beginning to gain momentum in RC-East. This had multiple effects: shadow insurgent governments were established, Afghan government officials were targeted, coalition officers' freedom of movement and contact with Afghans were reduced, and more effort had to go into combat operations. By 2005, popular support for local governments waned as infrastructure and services improved only marginally, and corruption increased. This hindered PRT efforts to build up local government. However, the teams' role in development increased significantly when tens of millions of dollars of CERP funds became available by 2007. This, in turn, increased the PRTs' ability to encourage local governments to take more responsibility for planning, coordination, and security—and prodding informal actors to cooperate with the formal Afghan government, which now had a say in large projects.

Reporting, Analysis, and Diplomatic Functions

PRTs played an important role as the "eyes and ears" for policymakers and officers in Kabul and Bagram. Much of this duty fell on State Department officers tasked with providing insights on political, social, and economic trends and the nature of rapidly morphing multiple insurgencies. This was important given that military intelligence tended to focus on gathering counterterrorism and combat information.

PRTs provided a steady stream of insights on local conditions to brigade and division commands and to NATO headquarters in Brussels. Since many Afghan government officials viewed PRT officers as neutral actors, they were in a position to provide credible information and analysis to both the GOA and policymakers in Washington, an important function given the complexity of Afghanistan.

The PRTs provided an opportunity to watch for corrupt officials, although the overall impact of this effort was marginal, given the difficulty of obtaining clear proof, coupled with Afghanistan's weak legal system. PRTs kept an eye on cross-border issues, including attacks and insurgents' attempts to extend influence into Afghanistan. The teams gradually built an understanding of tribal relations and disputes, a major issue in COIN operations. They disseminated current U.S. and ISAF policy positions and helped local government officials understand policy coming out of Kabul. Finally, PRT reporting was an extra "dissent channel" from the field, providing a sometimes-needed reality check to policy.

PRTs and USG Coordination

The Counterinsurgency Manual notes: "The political and military aspects of insurgencies are so bound together as to be inseparable," adding "The integration of civilian and military efforts is crucial to successful COIN operations. All efforts focus on supporting the local populace and host nation government. Political, social, and economic programs are usually more valuable than conventional military operations in addressing the root causes of conflict and undermining an insurgency."[57] PRTs knitted together political and military lines of operation while coordinating with the Afghan government. They were hubs for coordination at several levels (although it should be noted that in RC-East, the PRTs—with the exception of Panjshir—were effectively run by the military). Military officers within the PRTs provided a steady stream of insights on local conditions to brigade and division commands. State Department, USAID, and U.S. Department of Agriculture officers exchanged information and synchronized projects. More importantly, the PRTs served as platforms to reach out to local leaders and functioned as neutral sites for dispute resolution between forces in local society. For example, PRT Ghazni engaged as a neutral arbiter between the Pashtuns, Hazaras, Tajiks, and the nomadic Kuchis in that province.

The division of labor between the PRTs and the maneuver units differed between provinces, and over time. An example was Konar Province, where one of the battalion commanders noted "The [battalion] worked security, information operations, governance and economic development from the local population to the provincial level. The PRT worked government, economic development, information operations, and security from the provincial level to the local population."[58] Clearly this provided considerable overlap that needed coordination and teamwork.

The PRTs and brigade commands served as forums for coordination within the U.S. government interagency community. For example, in Nangarhar Province in 2008, they both coordinated counternarcotics efforts between the military, USAID, the State Department's INL, the Drug Enforcement Agency, and other players before further coordination with the Afghan government (although in this case much work was also done at the brigade level).[59] The PRTs also functioned almost as embassies, providing the infrastructure and planning for high-level visitors, including congressional delegations, Afghan officials, and military officers.

Strategic Benefits

As counter insurgency expert David Kilcullen notes, "In essence, effective counterinsurgency is a matter of good governance, backed by solid population security and economic development measures, resting on a firm foundation of energetic IO.[60] U.S. strategy often reflected this line of thinking, and PRTs helped provide the operational foundations in multiple ways: by building ties with the local population, by gaining knowledge of local politics and society, and by moving governance and basic justice systems forward. Although the results were uneven, PRTs engaged in public diplomacy campaigns, explaining the coalition presence and countering insurgent disinformation.

By supporting local government, PRTs contributed to the de facto decentralization of power in Afghanistan away from Kabul, with the strategic benefit of bringing decision making closer to the populations. This was not a defined PRT goal but rather a byproduct of their work with local authorities.

While they were expensive to operate, PRTs had the advantage of being much less costly than medium or large combat units. As Afghan police and military units expanded, PRTs provided an option to maintain a Coalition presence at a reduced cost. This was particularly important because part of the Taliban's strategy was to outlast the international presence. Viable because their operating costs were only a fraction of ISAF's overall operating expenses, PRTs gave countries with limited combat forces and budgets an opportunity to play a meaningful role. The successful New Zealand-led PRT in Bamian Province of RC-East, for example, maintained a platform in a strategically important province— given the Hazara ethnic minority in the province—while funding development projects, acting as a neutral arbiter of local disputes, and supporting Afghan security forces.

In their effort to expand governance, the teams benefitted from the grassroots democracy present in Pashtun society. In local or regional shuras (councils), discussions could go on for hours or days, often reaching consensus decisions that are binding, such as embracing the outcome of the 2004 elections, the National Solidarity Program, and related development councils that have been successful in some areas. The efforts of PRTs fit in well with the existing cultural tendency toward local, participatory democracy, and helped strengthen it.

PRTs also performed the less tangible function of providing an international presence at the local level. This was important in a tactical and strategic sense, because many Afghans, particularly those along the border with Pakistan, were "fence sitters," preferring to hedge their bets to see which faction would come out on top. Having a PRT presence gave the local population more confidence to side with the government while boosting the confidence of the local government, and made it harder for insurgents to fill any vacuums, particularly as the Taliban had as part of its strategy the establishment of shadow local governments.

Challenges PRTs Faced in RC-East

Provincial Reconstruction Teams faced a wide variety of challenges, some brought on by the complex environment in which they operated, some by the weakness of Afghan institutions, and some a result of flawed tactics, strategy, or misunderstandings of the situation on the ground. In a sense, given the very low level of development of Afghanistan, the teams were involved in construction, not reconstruction, and were misnamed as "reconstruction teams."

Provincial reconstruction teams in RC-East operated within a society that remained deeply traditional and conservative, particularly in areas where Pashtuns and Nuristanis lived. These societies were working through how they would adapt to encroaching modernity and outside influences, such as the role of women in society. The more conservative sectors of society wanted to put the brakes on change and, to some extent, development, which put them in opposition to the PRTs, whose officers wanted to push development forward. As noted previously, PRT officers' relatively short tours of duty (twelve to fifteen months) exacerbated this situation, which put pressure on them to get results quickly, despite the slow speed at which Afghan society often worked. Similarly, PRT efforts to build up government institutions encountered a system where personal relationships and personalities often mattered more than institutions and formal structures.

Efforts to build up local governance in provinces along the border encountered a harsh reality—insurgents had a very real capacity to assassinate government officials (as seen by the assassination of Paktia Governor Taniwal) or, at a minimum, hinder the steady development of local government and intimidate officials. This clearly challenged PRT effectiveness. Similarly, if the insurgency was seen as one large (if loosely affiliated) movement active in both Afghanistan and Pakistan, PRTs had the extremely difficult task of carrying out a COIN campaign in which they could directly influence only half of the population and geographic area of the insurgency. Education was a key to maintaining democracy, countering the ideology of the Taliban and other insurgent groups, and creating a workforce with employable skills. State education institutions were also critical of giving Afghan youths the option of studying in radical madrassas, and allowing them to become involved in the insurgency out of a lack of viable alternatives. Much of the young population appeared ready for positive social change. Aside from helping with infrastructure such as small schoolhouses, PRTs had only limited impact on the Afghan education system, which was almost nonexistent in 2001. There was an urgent need to build up a body of teachers and administrators, a task PRTs were not designed to do.

I returned to Afghanistan four times between the spring of 2003 and the spring of 2010, and each time it was clear that increased security measures had been put in place to protect U.S. personnel. They included bigger and more heavily armed convoys, with more armor coupled with more restrictions on travel. In effect, the insurgents achieved a COIN goal by incrementally separating the Coalition from the Afghan population, as we took reactive security measures. The perceived security threat also increased the troops' wariness, in some cases putting a wedge between them and the local population.

Selecting which provinces were to have PRTs and determining the level of resources the PRTs were to have, had strategic implications. For example, the PRT in Paktia initially covered Logar Province as well, and the PRT in Ghazni initially covered Wardak Province. This stretched the PRTs' resources, particularly given the difficulty of movement and the challenges of doing projects from a distance. This thin coverage worked well while the insurgency had limited capacity, but eventually provided an opportunity for the insurgents to increase their influence in Logar and Wardak, This had strategic implications, as these two provinces were adjacent to Kabul Province, and highways to the capital passed through them. Eventually, a Czech PRT arrived in Logar province, and a Turkish PRT was established in Wardak province, although both these countries had limited military, diplomatic, and development resources to deploy. Kapisa, a province to the east of Kabul that also had roads and hydropower facilities, initially received only limited attention, and eventually had a formidable insurgency take root. The remote province of Nuristan presented different challenges. Its remoteness, harsh winters, small population, and rugged mountain terrain made both civilian and military leaders reluctant to deploy a PRT, although one was eventually established. Similarly, the remote province of Daikundi was judged to have such limited strategic significance (along with a mostly Hazara population that was unfriendly to the Taliban) that a PRT had yet to be established by 2008, despite multiple requests from the governor.

As noted, a fundamental problem of U.S.-led PRTs (as well as battalions, brigades, and divisions) was the rapid rotation of staff into and out of Afghanistan, and the knowledge lost as a result. The complexity of Afghanistan and the rapid changes in the Afghan government, society, and the insurgency held back COIN advances. The rapid turnover of personnel also led to too-frequent changes of policies, as incoming officers made fundamental changes to their predecessor's policies and priorities. However, this situation improved as many military and civilian officers served multiple tours in Afghanistan, and the U.S. military established a program where officers would focus on Afghanistan and Pakistan. The difficulty the central government in Kabul had in developing coherent national policies for a country as diverse and rapidly changing as Afghanistan remained a challenge for embassies and national-level military commands.

Perhaps more important was the imbalance of civilian versus military personnel in PRTs. In part, this reflected the considerably greater resources of the Department of Defense in comparison to the State Department and USAID—as Kilcullen notes, "The U.S. Defense Department is about 210 times larger than the U.S. Agency for International Development and the State Department combined."[61] This held back COIN efforts. For example, in early 2005 this author worked for both the brigade and the PRT in Khost Province while at times covering Paktia and Paktika Provinces—a clear overstretch. With the appointment of Ambassador Holbrooke as the special representative for Afghanistan and Pakistan, this situation significantly improved, but imbalances remained.

Lessons Learned 2004–2008

While they PRTs did well operationally, they produced uneven results in some areas. Beginning in 2006, the increased amount of CERP funds moving through the PRTs in some provinces outpaced the teams' abilities to manage them. Some PRTs worked on women's rights issues, with mixed results—not surprisingly, given the extreme sensitivity of this issue, particularly in Pashtun areas. Although the PRTs had limited scope and legal authority to do so, they worked with the Afghan National Police—but could have done more, given the authority to do so. However, the shortcomings of the police, glaringly apparent by 2005, were beyond the capacity of the PRTs to address at the required scale. This mattered, in that the war in eastern Afghanistan between 2004 and 2008 was more a police war than an army war.

Similarly, the development of the judicial sector, an important part of countering the insurgents and developing Afghan civil society, lagged badly. Support for agriculture was weak, with limited USDA deployment and almost no funding. U.S. National Guard units eventually focused on agriculture, and increased USDA deployments under Ambassador Holbrooke—who recognized the fundamental importance of rural agriculture in Afghanistan—helped address this deficiency.

The limited attention paid to developing an overarching political strategy for RC-East and its provinces (in contrast to detailed military planning and strategizing) reduced the overall effectiveness of PRTs and the general COIN effort, at least until the last years of the decade. The time lost was hard to recover.

As the *Counterinsurgency Field Manual* notes, "PRTs were conceived as a means to extend the reach and enhance the legitimacy of the central government into the provinces of Afghanistan at a time when most assistance was limited to the nation's capital."[62]

The teams had some success in assisting the slowly forming central government to reach the provinces, but they also encountered a problem: what if some Afghans did not want the central government to reach them, because they were convinced that it was corrupt, inefficient, and/or dominated by members of a different ethnic group?

The COIN manual also notes, "The long-term goal is to leave a government able to stand by itself. In the end, the host nation has to win on its own. Achieving this requires development of viable local leaders and institutions."[63]

Due to a variety of factors, including years of war, massive civilian casualties, and an ensuing exodus of Afghans out of the country (plus the collapse of the education system under the Taliban), the base for a new civil service cadre was limited, and those who had the skills to run local government often preferred to live in Kabul or other large cities. PRTs could have done more to establish civil service academies at the provincial or regional level. However, did the Afghans have the will to build a government capable of standing on its own, while putting national interests ahead of personal, family, or tribal well-being? Did inherent divisions in Afghan society make any national cohesion or reconciliation impossible to achieve? Perhaps most unsettling of all, what if the international community, particularly the United States, wanted this nation-building effort to succeed more than Afghans did?

Conclusions on PRTs 2004–2008

During 2004–2008, PRTs were successful as joint civil military hubs that extended the reach of government, implemented development projects, helped stabilize RC-East, and served as multipurpose COIN platforms. While they had flaws—with the lack of an adequate civilian presence being one of the most apparent—they adapted well, and the increased attention and resources given to Afghanistan under the Obama administration increased their utility. Clearly, PRTs contributed to an overall successful COIN effort in RC-East during this period. The fact that there was no large-scale internally based insurgency against the coalition and the Afghan government in RC-East between 2004 and 2008 underscores this success. Coalition efforts often forced insurgent groups to operate from outside of the area, allowing local government to take root in many places.

PRTs also laid the foundation for the expansion of the civilian "surge" begun under Ambassador Holbrooke in 2009. Not only was much of the necessary infrastructure already in place, but previous experience was brought to bear in terms of priorities, staffing, best practices, and Afghan acceptance of PRT methods. Similarly, the PRT presence helped the Afghan IDLG, newly formed in late 2007, extend its operations to the provincial and district levels, an important factor in building the governance "pillar" of COIN.

Importantly, the PRTs provided some stability and breathing room as local government established itself and began to function. They helped develop local leaders, an important initiative given the dearth of trained civil servants, and the importance of credible local government. This was mostly an ad-hoc effort, but methods included funding salaries for the governor's staff, providing transportation, training to perform basic administration, and giving advice as requested. One success story was the very capable and courageous Gulab Mangal, who eventually became Governor of Helmand Province, after having worked closely with Coalition forces on development, security and political issues as Governor of Paktika and Laghman Provinces.

PRTs provided what the Taliban and other insurgent groups could not offer—development projects, including major road projects, a steady stream of improvements to infrastructure, and the prospect of a better future. This gave the coalition an asymmetric advantage over the Taliban and other insurgent groups, given the stark poverty of many areas. Small-scale projects carried out immediately after combat operations, including the repair of infrastructure damaged during operations, were also important COIN tools.

The PRTs informally adopted the "ink spot" approach to counterinsurgency, where security, governance, and development expanded outward from a central location, pushing out the insurgents. In most cases, the center of the ink spot was the provincial capital, usually the largest town and the economic and government hub. PRTs were based in these capitals and provided some of the money, political support and, to a limited extent, the security to fuel the expansion of the ink spot.

The clear, coherent military chain of command, with brigade commands providing direction and oversight—while still giving

PRT commanders the authority to adjust to local conditions—helped the PRTs succeed. Adaptations in the control and auditing of CERP funds over time improved this program, and helped show Afghans that this money was being spent responsibly.

Developments late in this period (and afterwards) improved Coalition support for local governance. The deployment of District Support Teams (DSTs) extended the PRT concept to the district level, an important step in building local governance. The District Delivery Program, intended to build up local government in key districts (see Annex 1), particularly after combat operations, was an important initiative to provide resources at the district level. A Senior Civilian Representative (SCR) position was created to coordinate civilian agencies in RC-East, provide a comprehensive political and development strategy at the provincial/regional level, and manage critical civilian-military relationships—an important step forward.

While the PRTs in eastern Afghanistan made significant contributions during this period, in the end, success or failure depended on the Afghans and their ability to stem corruption, develop credible leaders, heal rifts between ethnic and tribal groups, resist insurgents and negative foreign influences, and put the good of the nation above narrower interests. These were factors that outweighed any impact the PRTs could make.

Analysis of Security and PRTs

RC-East dealt with a wide variety of conditions in terms of security, economic development, Afghan government capacity, ethnic groups, insurgent capabilities, border conditions, and terrain. As a result, each PRT was considerably different than other PRTs and was specifically adapted to the conditions and development needs of its province. The most important variable was the level of security (for a more detailed discussion, see Annex IV). This determined not only how much access the PRTs had to their districts—some were no-go areas—, but also what type and how many development projects were undertaken. One measure of the long-term success of the PRT concept in Afghanistan will be the rate of shift in focus from security concerns to reconstruction and political efforts. This depends on a multitude of factors—how strong and effective the Afghan security forces eventually become, whether the Taliban and other insurgent groups are able to continue their activities, overall economic development, the maturation of the district, provincial and national government, the future level of NGO and international organization involvement, the rejection of the insurgents by the populace, and events in the FATA. Ultimately, the PRTs will completely hand the "humanitarian space" off to the NGOs, IOs, and the GOA. At that point, the PRTs will have worked themselves out of a job.

PRTs in Other Times and Places

The basic concept of PRTs could transfer to other countries with insurgencies, where there is a need to extend the reach of the government and for civilian-military coordination. Indeed, the U.S. introduced the concept in Iraq after seeing how well the PRTs performed in Afghanistan. If PRTs reduce the need for the costly deployment of combat units, they make sense as a money-saving option. Partnered with police forces, PRTs are certainly less expensive than maneuver units, and can stay in place for years—an important consideration for countering insurgencies, which often go on for years. They may also have relevance for "nation-building" efforts that do not necessarily have an active insurgency to confront, or for post-conflict situations—for example, the PRT model could support elections in post-conflict countries.

PRTs provided civilian and military officers practical, hard-won expertise in how to conduct a counterinsurgency. They were a valuable aset for the United States, and the concept and the expertise to run them should be retained through USAID, State, and parts of the military that will be involved in future counterinsurgencies, such as Civil Affairs units, Special Forces and the Marines Corps.

The Role of Provincial Reconstruction Teams 97

Officers from the Khost Provincial Reconstruction Team meet with local Pashtun leaders, Khost, winter of 2004.

Children, Khost Province, 2004.

Waiting for attention at a Medcap (Medical Civil Action Program), Khost Province, 2005.

Khost PRT commander Maj. Carl Hollister, with Afghan staff, 2005.

9

The Afghanistan-Pakistan Border

The border area between Afghanistan and Pakistan is a key factor in both the international community's counterinsurgency strategy, and the long-term stability of the Afghan government. The rugged topography, the fact that the Pashtuns live on both sides of the border, and a local economy based, in part, on smuggling makes it extremely challenging to control the flow of insurgents, drugs, and goods across this border. During the period 2004–2008, the U.S. worked with the Afghan government to increase security along this border, establishing firebases while also building up the ANA, the ANP, and the ABP. To improve cooperation with Pakistani security forces, Border Control Centers and Border Flag meetings, along with some common means of radio communication, were established. More technical measures such as sensors and surveillance can provide only partial solutions, and the sheer number of troops and police that would be required to effectively seal the border make this an unlikely and unsustainable option. Improving security and standards of living along this border will require long-term effort, including cooperation between the Afghan and Pakistani governments at the national and local levels, coupled with sustained international assistance in development, governance, security, and counternarcotics.

This chapter will examine the geographic, security, social, and commercial aspects of the Afghanistan-Pakistan border area in RC-East during this time. Specifically, what security steps did the Afghan government take to secure its border? How did the U.S government support this effort? Where and how did political-military cooperation with Pakistani forces take place along the border? How did the policies and actions of Pakistan's security forces and government affect counterinsurgency efforts in RC-East during this period? What were the lessons learned?

Nature of the Border Regions

Seen from the air, or even up close on the ground, the location of the border between Afghanistan and Pakistan in RC-East is often difficult to determine. While the Spin Ghar mountains between Nangarhar Province and Kurram Agency provide a clear dividing line, in other places the border is a more arbitrary line through low, rugged hills, easily crossed via countless paths and jeep tracks. Light and medium weapons are abundant, particularly after the serial wars of the last decades. Close to the border, the population tends to be "fence sitters," waiting to see which side will prevail before becoming allied with one side or another.

The ABP is responsible for border security, which includes countering smuggling, drug trafficking, and the infiltration of insurgents. In the east (ABP Zone 2), the ABP was assigned an end-strength goal of 4,200 men to control the border and a zone fifty kilometers into Afghanistan, with an initial training period of eight weeks at the Regional Training Centers. The U.S. Army's 173rd Airborne Brigade, based out of Jalalabad, began a small program to mentor and train some ABP units in 2007. By October 2008 the more formal Focused Border Development Program was established in RC-East by the U.S. military to provide additional training, equipping and mentoring. However, the ABP remained a fairly weak force, hindered to some extent by lack of equipment and training, and seemingly of lower priority than the ANA and ANP. It also faced logistical and support challenges at its more remote border posts. Some ABP units were also posted relatively far from the border—in Paktika, the ABP provincial commander at one point kept much of his force in the town of Orgun-E, away from contested border areas.

Informal groups also played a security role along the border, particularly early in this period. For example, the 24th Afghan Militia Force in Khost province had several hundred men under arms, although by 2005, the Coalition's Disbandment of Illegal Armed

Border Provinces of Regional Command East and the Adjacent FATA

Groups (DIAG) program had demobilized most of these groups, and the ANA increasingly took control. Many tribal groups could organize small, armed *alberkai* groups to carry out specific security tasks. During the elections of 2004 and 2005, these *alberkai* were often effective in providing local security at polling stations in border provinces. In addition, tribal militias at times prevented the transit of insurgents through their areas.

During the period 2004–2008, cross-border attacks into Afghanistan were fairly common in Khost, Paktika, Paktia and Konar provinces, and ranged in size from small groups to upward of fifty fighters, as well as rocket attacks and the setting of IEDs.

In contrast, attacks from Afghanistan into Pakistan were, in the author's experience, very rare. Arrayed along the Afghan side of the border in 2004 was a thin force of U.S. conventional and Special Forces, some ANP, and a very limited number of ANA. At the same time, by the spring of 2005, the insurgency began gaining momentum, increasing its numbers, weaponry and ability to carry out operations.

The U.S., in coordination with the Afghan government, established and maintained a string of firebases in the border provinces of RC-East. Many of these were subject to attacks by insurgent forces. In the author's experience in Khost and Paktika provinces during the period 2004–2005, the attackers at times numbered more than fifty, and were repulsed by small arms, often augmented by artillery and close air support, resulting in considerable enemy casualties. Many insurgents were operating from the adjacent North Waziristan agency in Pakistan, where the town of Miram Shah was an insurgent center, according to numerous press reports. Despite the high insurgent casualties, attacks using similar tactics were repeated. Some of these attacks may have been training exercise for new recruits, while some may have been to demonstrate military activity to the insurgent's backers. An additional factor might have been that overrunning one of these firebases would have been enough of a "win," particularly in propaganda terms, that the insurgents judged it to be worth the casualties.

These firebases almost certainly hindered attacks further into border provinces and further north by acting as a "magnet" for attackers, while making it difficult for large groups to move across the border. However, these small bases couldn't effectively stop infiltration by individual insurgents who (unless they were Arabs, Chechens or other foreigners) could blend in with the local population, and then regroup within Afghanistan. This remains a problem—a U.S. civilian officer based in Khost in 2010 described the border in that province as a "sieve" with the insurgents able to cross the border easily.[64]

Further to the north in the border provinces of Nangarhar, Laghman, Nuristan, and Konar (known as N2KL during this period, several joint U.S.-Afghan checkpoints were operating at major infiltration routes along the border. Similar to Khost, this border was difficult to control due to the rugged terrain, the numerous trails and paths that led to the border, an active insurgency, and a population that acted in the interests of self-preservation while calculating the relative strengths of opposing forces. Posts such as "Checkpoint Delta" were located in natural passes through the mountains, where it was easiest for the insurgents to move people and material through. These outposts served to hinder these flows, collect information, and force insurgents to use more difficult routes, and were often effective COIN tools.

In N2KL CERP funded connector roads and bridges (particularly over the Konar river) leading to the border with Pakistan. These served multiple purposes: increasing the mobility of military forces, promoting cross-border trade, and serving as farm-to-market roads. An additional intent was to "funnel" insurgents into these more easily monitored and controlled routes,—while flagging potential insurgents choosing instead to use trails and paths. To the north, the high mountains of Nuristan made border control quite difficult but also presented challenges to infiltrating insurgents.

During this period, the Border Management Task Force (BMTF) within the U.S. embassy had four core responsibilities:[65] mentor operations; provision of equipment and infrastructure; coordination of a border control and border security strategies both within the USG and with the GOA and ISAF; and, along with the European Commission, the coordination of international donors. One of the BMTF's main areas of focus in RC-East was the crossing at Torkham Gate in Nangarhar Province, where they posted mentors to the Afghan Border Police and Afghan Customs. While the BMTF's efforts yielded positive results, their overall staffing during this period seemed inadequate relative to the scale of their tasks.

Economic Factors of the Border

Local economies in Afghan border provinces had strong commercial ties across the border, with some Pakistani towns acting as market and service hubs for Afghans. Pakistani rupees were used as a parallel currency. While most of this informal trade was benign, there was also considerable smuggling of merchandise, drugs, timber and gems from Afghanistan into Pakistan. One of the driving factors was the Afghan Transit Trade Agreement, originally signed in 1965, and updated in June 2011. This agreement allowed some goods to be imported duty-free into Afghanistan for use there, but created a strong incentive to smuggle these items back into Pakistan at a profit. The drug trade also drove cross-border smuggling, with precursor chemicals coming into Afghanistan, and opium, heroin, and hashish moving in the opposite direction. Although poppy production in RC-East was small relative to southern Afghanistan, in some years Nangarhar had a significant crop, and labs in this province refined raw opium apparently brought from other parts of Afghanistan.

Within RC-East, by far the most important border crossing was Torkham Gate, where the road from Peshawar goes through the Khyber Pass and into Afghanistan, continuing on to Jalalabad, Kabul, and eventually central Asia. Torkham was also one of two major entry points for ISAF supplies landed in Karachi. By 2008 infrastructure on the Afghan side of the border crossing had been expanded considerably, with buildings for customs and immigration officials; truck inspection bays; a nearby ISAF firebase; a trilateral coordination center; and a large, chaotic informal sector of vehicle repair shops, truck stops, gas stations, and food stalls.

On any given day, the traffic of trucks, cars, and pedestrians through Torkham was substantial, with perhaps 20,000 people crossing daily, posing both opportunities and challenges. Customs and transit fees were a potentially rich source of revenue for Kabul, a fact noted by many in the international community who pressed for more efficient collection. During the period 2004– 2009, it was rumored that some of this money remained in Nangarhar, bolstering the local economy and infrastructure. Biometrics were only beginning to be implemented by 2008, along with any sort of immigration database.

Pakistan as a Factor

The reality of a largely artificial border dividing the Pashtuns, coupled with closely related and linked insurgencies on both sides of the border, meant that events in Pakistan had a very direct impact on Afghanistan. This, and the issue of sanctuaries, has been well documented by various authors.⁶⁶ The Frontier Corps traditionally had responsibility for much of the border in the FATA across from Afghanistan, although by 2002 the Pakistani military (PAKMIL) had also become engaged. Importantly, the traditional influence of tribal leaders diminished quickly as insurgents assassinated many of them, and the long-standing system of political agents lost influence. In addition to some military operations, the PAKMIL negotiated peace agreements with insurgents, including the "Shakai agreement" signed in April 2004 in South Waziristan. This was largely ineffectual, while raising concerns among some U.S. military officers in Afghanistan that it would allow the insurgents to focus on cross-border attacks. The PAKMIL signed a further agreement with North Waziristan insurgents in September 2006. By 2008, the PAKMIL, politicians and many citizens came to the realization that insurgents presented a threat to the Pakistani state and society, spurring large military operations in South Waziristan, Bajaur and Swat.

Cross-border Cooperation and Multilateral Efforts

During this period, several mechanisms were established to coordinate with Pakistani security forces. Border Coordination Centers (BCCs) were agreed to; the first was built just inside Afghanistan in 2008 at Torkham. It was manned by Pakistani, Afghan, and U.S. officers. Looking like fortified Quonset huts, the BCCs provided a node intended to exchange information and reduce accidental clashes along the border. Border flag meetings to exchange information and establish personal relations at the brigade and battalion levels were held. Frequencies for radio communications were designated so that officers on either side of the border could talk in emergencies. At a higher level, in 2003 the Tripartite Commission was established as "a joint forum on military and security issues which brings together representatives from the NATO-led ISAF operation, Afghanistan, and Pakistan."⁶⁷ In practice, these arrangements were far from perfect. Meetings were cancelled for various reasons, radio calls at times went unanswered, agreements were not followed up on, considerable suspicions existed, and national interests clearly did not always coincide. However, putting these channels in place was a necessary step, and yielded benefits.

On the political side, some governors maintained informal contacts with their Pakistani counterparts.[68] The first "Peace Jirga" in August 2007 brought together roughly 700 elders from both countries (a direct result of a September 2006 dinner hosted by President Bush for Musharraf and Karzai), as an attempt to resolve issues through more traditional methods. Afghans in the border provinces during this period, in the author's experience, often harbored considerable resentment towards the government of Pakistan (as distinct from Pakistanis) over what they perceived as Pakistan's fueling of violence in border provinces of Afghanistan. These hard feelings were exacerbated by the strong rhetoric of leaders on both sides of the border, blaming the other side for security problems.

Relevance of Border Issues to U.S. Objectives in Afghanistan

This border is a determining factor in the future of the international community's programs in governance, security, economic assistance, and narcotics control in both Afghanistan and Pakistan. Establishing local governance will remain a challenge, as government officials will be under threat—and some civil servants will avoid these postings in favor of safer, more comfortable jobs in Kabul. The local population, already skeptical of the government, may be further intimidated into withholding its support. Elections will be more difficult to hold, and more costly due to security overhead. International development projects will continue to face significant security costs, and international experts will be less likely to develop the necessary in-depth knowledge of the border areas. In the long run, the GOA will not have sufficient revenue to field the necessary security forces along the border; the international community will need to determine what support levels it will sustain, and donor fatigue may set in. Finally, one of Afghanistan's significant economic advantages—its location along trade routes, as well as along potential gas pipeline and electrical power line routes from Central Asia—will provide the government less revenue from transit fees and customs revenues if this area remains insecure.

Afghanistan-Pakistan Border: Lessons Learned

Securing the border along RC-East is a daunting task, with many variables that may not change. The rugged terrain, the fact that the Pashtuns live on both sides of a largely artificial dividing line, and the disinclination of the local population to be ruled over or controlled are factors that will not change. Smuggling opportunities, brought on by a more or less open border and the limited reach of both the Afghan and Pakistani governments, may change to some degree over the long run. How countries in the region (and private donors from the Persian Gulf) act to promote their national or ideological interests are major factors that will remain. The planned drawdown of international troops from Afghanistan will make the border even more fluid. What does this imply?

Technological solutions for partially sealing the border—sensors, camera systems, and fences have been proposed—will not be effective due to the sheer number of routes across the border, the physical ruggedness of the area, the amount of manpower required to react to alarms, and the number of people who regularly move between the two countries. —Minefields—which would not be effective for similar reasons—would result in considerable civilian casualties and the death of livestock, and would be unpopular in Afghanistan, where there are still millions of landmines laid by the Soviets. High-tech aerial surveillance, including aerostats, has positively changed the equation, but still requires resources to analyze data and react to alerts. Moreover, in almost all cases, cross-border strikes by soldiers will be counterproductive, given the predictably negative public reaction.

The case in which border security becomes less effective—and governance is weak—would hinder licit cross-border trade, reduce investment, and slow the development of infrastructure (roads, electricity, and water) that are needed to move border societies forward. Weak border security is advantageous to criminal groups, drug traffickers, and insurgents. These factors could feed a cycle in which as the border becomes increasingly more difficult to govern and provide services to, it becomes more unstable.

Rapid social changes are underway that will change the nature of the border region. Roads are opening up previously isolated, localized societies; very rapid advances in telecommunications (particularly cell phones and the internet) are having a similar effect, and many Pashtuns have travelled outside of the border areas as businessmen, migrants (including a large population in Karachi), refugees, or overseas guest workers. The considerable presence of aid workers and foreign military over the last decades has also had an impact on local societies. These trends, complex and ongoing, may lend themselves to more government influence, and international assistance.

In the best-case scenario, improved education and justice systems, and more representative governments providing essential services could influence the border tribes and societies. Although the achievement of any one of these three factors is far from certain and will require years to achieve, it could lay a foundation for improved local and regional stability. Similarly, microeconomic improvement—in the form of more (legal) jobs providing steady incomes—would clearly be a stabilizing factor. In the end, the direction and speed of change in the border areas will depend heavily on the local population—what they judge to be in their collective interests (and if they can reach consensus on this); what changes take place internal to their societies, including the role of women and young leaders; and their perception of who will prevail in the current conflicts.

Some of these changes will be generational and slow, requiring "strategic patience" on the part of the international community, and Islamabad and Kabul. This argues for planning cycles that look forward ten to fifteen years, with assistance redesigned to provide less on a yearly basis, but extended over a longer timeline. Maintaining this flow will almost certainly become more difficult, as the international commitments to Afghanistan becomes reduced, troop levels are reduced, and overall development budgets of western countries are cut back. To justify this commitment, the government of Afghanistan and local communities must ensure that funds are used well, while showing results that clearly benefit donors.

The Afghanistan-Pakistan Border

Attack helicopter flies over Paktika Province near the border with Pakistan, 2005.

10

Nangarhar Case Study: Progress in COIN and Counternarcotics

Nangarhar Province showed considerable progress in counterinsurgency, counternarcotics, local governance and development during the period 2004–2008. These successes were the result of several factors, including the considerable efforts and resources of the U.S. military, other U.S. agencies, coalition partners, parts of the Afghan government, and local tribes and leaders. Although what worked there was not necessarily replicable in other provinces, given Afghanistan's considerable diversity, some of the strategies seemed relevant beyond Nangarhar, particularly interagency coordination.

Although the security situation was tenuous in 2004, by 2008 it had improved dramatically to where Afghan security forces had the lead in the province. Local governance, at the provincial level, was forming and implementing policies. The economy expanded, especially agriculture, small businesses, trade, and, in some years, the illicit production of opium.

During the 2004-5 growing seasons in Nangarhar, the poppy crop was considerably reduced, and during 2007-8, it was almost eliminated as various factors converged. The rapid growth of the licit economy gave people alternatives to growing poppy or trafficking in opium. The government, mullahs, and to some extent, the tribes encouraged farmers not to grow poppy. Increased security by 2007 allowed the police, army, and eradication units to reliably operate through much of the province. The appointment of a strong governor who implemented an aggressive counternarcotics strategy also helped.

Another significant factor in Nangarhar's progress was improved coordination among U.S. government agencies and the U.S.

military. This cooperation yielded by mid-2008 "Nangarhar Inc.," an attempt to integrate COIN, counternarcotics, and development strategies into one long-term plan. At the same time, U.S. agencies completed a "synchronization matrix" for counternarcotics. Both of these efforts benefited from the planning capability of the 173rd ABCT's plans section in 2008.

This chapter will describe in detail how COIN was carried out in Nangarhar during this period.

Background on Nangarhar Province

Nangarhar Province is located east of Kabul, along the border with Pakistan, and at the western end of the Khyber Pass. The province has two major rivers, the Kabul and the Konar, which flow year-round and support local agriculture, the province's economic bedrock. Most of the population, including those who live in the capital city of Jalalabad, reside in the irrigated plains along these rivers. To the south, the Spin Ghar Mountain Range reaching more than 14,000 feet makes infiltration from Pakistan difficult, especially in the winter. The road linking Kabul to Peshawar, a major paved highway and a historical trade route, crosses the province from east to west. There is one paved airstrip in Jalalabad, although it is primarily for military use.

The population, which is almost entirely Pashtun, is divided into several main tribes. The only other major ethnic group, the Peshaei, is present in the northwest of the province. The population has been increasing because of natural growth and the return of refugees, mostly from Pakistan. Nangarhar is in a strategic location due to the regional trade route and because it borders three sections of the FATA. It is also the political and economic hub for the surrounding provinces due to existing trade routes, its relatively large population, geography, and Afghan history. The former king's winter palace is located in Nangarhar, and to this day, Kabul pays attention to the province's circumstances.

Because the province's central valley along the Kabul River is at a relatively low altitude, the climate is hot in the summer and mild during the winter. This climate and an extensive irrigation system, largely installed by the Soviets, allow farmers to grow up to three crops a year, mostly wheat, rice, sugar cane, fruits, vegetables, and poppy in some years.

COIN Strategy in Nangarhar

The COIN strategy for Nangarhar had three main "pillars": security, economic development, and governance. Complementary efforts included public relations and information operations, counternarcotics, rule of law (which could be included under the governance pillar), and counterterrorism (which could be included under security).

Security Considerations

From 2004 to 2008, the ANA and coalition forces increased their presence in Nangarhar, and the ANP and the ABP showed progress. Insurgent groups had only a limited capacity to carry out operations and held very little territory in the province. Although coalition forces remained mostly within the NATO command structure, Nangarhar was almost exclusively an area for U.S. efforts.

Importantly, the population supported the ANA and was generally in favor of the coalition presence. Locals supported the provincial government despite many complaints, and some backed President Karzai's national administration. The Taliban did not appear to have much popular support, although this could be hard to judge because locals probably told coalition officers what they wanted to hear. An attempt by the Taliban to establish a consolidated front (the so-called "Tora Bora Front") in southern Nangarhar in late 2007 was soundly defeated. Because of this inability to confront Afghan and coalition forces, the Taliban resorted to asymmetric tactics, such as improvised explosive devices and car bombs, in Jalalabad and district centers.

Significantly, the Nangarhar tribes could muster their own forces, and in some cases prevented the Taliban from crossing their territory. Some tribes, such as the Mohmand and the Afridi, had populations on both sides of the border with Pakistan and influenced how much control the Afghan state had over the border. During 2004 and 2005, local militias, particularly that of Peshaei leader Hazrat Ali, had significant influence.

Civilian casualties were a source of considerable tension between coalition forces and the local population. The so-called "Marsof incident" of 2007 involving a U.S. Marine Corps Special Operations Company, during which more than two dozen civilians died, was a considerable setback for relations with the local community. Aerial bombings that caused unintended casualties, such as the erroneous attack on a wedding in 2008, also increased tensions. Besides basic moral concerns, civilian casualties needed to be avoided due to the elevated place of revenge in Pashtun culture (deaths of family members can set off decades-long feuds) and the difficulty in rebuilding positive relations with the community afterwards.

Internal Afghan tensions also presented security challenges. The riots in Jalalabad during the spring of 2005 were one example. Instigators hijacked an isolated protest by university students and turned it into several days of rioting that included attacks against the UN office and the Pakistani consulate.

The Coalition presence began with Special Forces and a PRT in 2003. The Marines established a battalion-level presence in the winter of 2004-2005, followed by a brigade headquarters at Jalalabad Airfield covering Nangarhar and the nearby provinces of Konar, Laghman, and Nuristan (previously, Nangarhar had been supervised by the brigade headquarters in Khost). In 2007 and 2008, a Special Troops Battalion (composed mostly of support units, particularly engineers) provided excellent security and coordination with the PRT and Afghan forces. ANA presence also increased with a brigade headquarters under the Kabul-based corps command.

As the U.S. and Afghan military gained strength, small firebases and patrol bases were established.. These small bases increased the security of the rural population, supported the local security forces, and put U.S. forces in contact with more of the population. While these small bases proved vulnerable to attack in nearby provinces, particularly Nuristan, in Nangarhar they were fairly secure. Probably the most important base was at Torkham Gate, which eventually expanded to include a BCC that housed Afghan, Pakistani, and U.S. officers.

U.S. military units in Nangarhar worked to develop Afghan Army and ANP units, conducted combined patrols, provided equipment, and mentored Afghan officers at various levels up to brigade staff. Coalition officers also worked to improve coordination between different Afghan security forces, which often lacked compatible communications or had considerable animosity toward each other. The establishment of a joint control center in Jalalabad brought together U.S. and Afghan security forces to coordinate responses to security incidents.

The ANP were a weak link in the security forces in Nangarhar. While the Afghan Army enjoyed popular support and was a source of national pride, the population saw the ANP as providing limited security at best, and being corrupt and predatory at worst. A major U.S. effort to bolster the ANP began in 2005 with a "regional training center" east of Jalalabad. Nangarhar also benefited from a relatively competent provincial police chief appointed in January 2007. The nascent ABP was being developed during this period, but was not yet fully staffed, funded, or equipped.

Economic Development: Steady Expansion

Nangarhar's economy strengthened over this four-year period, although statistics were far from complete. This was a result of the improved security that allowed markets to be established, while assistance from CERP, USAID, the Asian Development Bank, and the European Union helped expand the economy. In addition, the growing U.S. military presence injected funds into the local economy and provided jobs.

The increased trade to and from Pakistan (including considerable NATO logistical movements into Afghanistan through Torkham) provided various types of employment, and tariffs imposed at the border helped support the Nangarhar provincial government. Although difficult to quantify, poppy proceeds clearly boosted the local economy, as did a brisk trade of smuggled consumer goods into Pakistan from the trade agreements allowing goods to enter Afghanistan with reduced tariffs. More importantly, there existed a strong entrepreneurial bent among the local population. However, many economic challenges remained. The lack of electricity was a major hurdle—as a comparison, the generators at JAF produced more electricity than was available in the rest of the province. Only the ingenuity of Afghan technicians held together the antiquated

Soviet-era generators at the Darunta Dam just west of Jalalabad. Equally daunting for the business world was the weak rule of law, while the system of property records often had overlapping deeds from different periods, further hindering business. The irrigation system suffered from lack of maintenance, although by the spring of 2008, CERP funds were being used to hire locals to repair it.

Politics of Nangarhar and COIN

Multiple poles of power, both within the local government and through informal actors such as tribal leaders, powerful families and business leaders, made Nangarhar politics very complex. Combined with this was the disruption caused by decades of war, the influence of the Karzai administration on local politics, the influence and political relations of the coalition, drug money, and the influence of foreign players. The province's turbulent history affected local politics as well, through long-standing tribal disputes coupled with persistent memories of who sided with which faction during Afghanistan's wars that began with the 1979 Soviet invasion.

Two governors played major roles during this time. Hajji Din Mohammad was influential as a member of a prominent old family of Nangarhar and an ally of Karzai's. Later the governor of Kabul Province, he was affable, shrewd, and charming, but had limited popular support, and some Afghans felt he was unduly influenced by Pakistan. The second influential governor was Gul Agha Sherzai, formerly the governor of Kandahar Province, where he had considerable sway. He was a forceful man known as the "Bulldozer," who developed a reputation for getting things done, despite the lack of a local power base upon his arrival. The presidential election of 2004 and the parliamentary elections of 2005 went relatively smoothly in Nangarhar, and the local population largely saw the results as credible.

Overall, provincial government expanded during this period and the Jalalabad municipality was able to provide some services. By 2008, some government was present in each of the province's 22 districts, but was uneven in quality and capacity. The 2005 elections elected provincial councils, but in Nangarhar, (as in other provinces) it had almost no funding, and its powers and authorities were not well-defined. During the period 2007-2008, the provincial council attempted to be a counterbalance to Governor Sherzai and his policies, with mixed results.

Most political parties had been largely discredited among the population, who saw the parties as having a role in the power struggles that contributed to Afghanistan's wars. Only two parties were influential in Nangarhar during this time, either overtly or covertly: the Hezb-e Islami Khalis, created by now deceased former mujahedeen leader Younus Khalis; and the HIG of opposition leader Gulbuddin Hekmatyar, who lived in exile in Pakistan.

Counternarcotics in Nangarhar

Nangarhar has historically been a major poppy-growing area of Afghanistan. The poppy is planted in the late fall, then harvested in April or May, depending on the altitude. The 2008 United Nations Office on Drugs and Crime report for Afghanistan said that : "Nangarhar was traditionally a large poppy growing area, and in 2007 was estimated to have 18,739 hectares of opium cultivation. In 2008, Nangarhar became poppy free for the first time since the UN began opium cultivation monitoring in Afghanistan. In 2004, opium cultivation in Nangarhar was 28,213 hectares; in 2005, it fell to 1,093 hectares. In 2006, cultivation increased to 4,872 hectares but could only be found in very remote parts of the province."[69]

The reduction of poppy in the 2004–2005 growing season was due to the convergence of many factors. First, farmers believed large-scale eradication operations were imminent, and were reluctant to plant as a result. Second, growers anticipated that both the Afghan and U.S. governments had large-scale development projects in the pipeline that would provide alternative livelihoods and jobs. Third, the Afghan government at the local and national level campaigned publicly against poppy cultivation. Fourth, local mullahs preached that drug production was against Islam.

As noted, however, poppy cultivation increased in the next two growing seasons (2006-2007, and 2009-2010). As a result, Governor Sherzai led an aggressive counternarcotics campaign beginning in the fall of 2007, with support from U.S. agencies. His government put growers in jail, and worked with district governors and tribal leaders to reduce the poppy crop. At the same time, the mullahs again spoke out against drug production. Helicopter overflights of Nangarhar in the spring of 2008 showed almost no poppy,[70] an astonishing outcome. At the same time, poppy production in neighboring Konar, Laghman, and Nuristan provinces was less than 1,000 hectares each.

While the Afghan government can rightly take most of the credit for this success, U.S. efforts also contributed. The U.S. Drug Enforcement Agency and the State Department's International Narcotics and Law Enforcement Bureau were both active in Nangarhar, and the U.S. military supported security to the point where the Afghan police were able to operate in most districts (in contrast to provinces such as Helmand). The establishment of small bases, in particular, helped extend security to the districts, and the Taliban was unable to take and hold areas that could have benefited the narcotics traffickers.

The construction of farm-to-market roads to bring licit crops to markets was important, as were efforts by U.S. Department of Agriculture officers to form agricultural cooperatives in 2005. A particularly daunting problem was microcredit, since many poor farmers were growing poppy in order to pay off loans from drug-connected intermediaries.

The plans section of the U.S. Army 173rd ABCT hosted a series of interagency meetings on counternarcotics beginning in the fall of 2007. These meetings produced a synchronization matrix of U.S. counternarcotics efforts for the province, determining which agency was doing what, where, and for what end, while also providing a forum for discussions. This effort identified overlaps and gaps, and informed the planning for Nangarhar Inc. (discussed later) as well.

Conditions specific to Nangarhar Province contributed to counternarcotics "wins" in both the 2004-2005 and 2007-2008 growing seasons. Chief among these were alternatives to poppy production that created jobs in agriculture (the climate allows several crops a year), small businesses (especially in Jalalabad), and trade along the route with Pakistan through the Khyber Pass. Large infrastructure projects such as road-building and irrigation systems supported counternarcotics efforts by providing alternative jobs to working in the poppy fields or labs, such as construction jobs for unskilled or semiskilled laborers. Improved security extended to many rural areas, police were able to move more freely, and as a result assistance projects were implemented in more districts. Small firebases contributed to this improvement by creating secure areas in some districts. In turn, advances in economic development and governance almost certainly supported the security "pillar."

While difficult to quantify, counternarcotics successes supported COIN efforts. The reduced poppy crop meant less money to fund the insurgency, and almost certainly reduced the level of corruption in the government. In a more general sense, the public saw that laws were being enforced and that the government was engaged and having an impact. Interagency cooperation, not only at the strategic level but also at the operational level, was vital.

The efforts of Governor Sherzai were critical for the counternarcotics effort of 2007–2008. In most provinces, the governor is the most important local official; having a governor committed to the counternarcotics effort, and influential enough to carry out a program, was indispensable. However, there were no convictions of major Nangarhar-based drug producers/traffickers during this period. The judiciary, and the apparent lack of will by the Afghan national government to go after traffickers, was a weak link in counternarcotics efforts.

The reduction or elimination of poppy meant a very significant loss of income for what, in most cases, were poor communities. Particularly during the period 2004–2005, communities reduced their crop with the understanding that there would be a "payoff" in terms of jobs or projects—and if this payoff did not come through, it was clear that parts of the rural population would turn against the government and the Coalition. It was critical that the Coalition follow through on any such compact. Farmers may have been adopting a strategy of not growing poppy during years when they perceived that the risk of eradication was high. Because opium gum can be stored for several years, this may have given them an economic "cushion" to make it through these years. A long-term, integrated strategy that planned for several years (and made multiyear commitments) was necessary. Nangarhar Inc. discussed in the next section, was such a strategy.

Nangarhar Inc. as an Integrated Plan

"Nangarhar Inc." was an integrated, long-term development and commercial plan for Nangarhar to support both counterinsurgency and counternarcotics efforts. This plan was informally initiated in late 2007 by the commander of the 173rd ABCT; the State Department political advisor to the brigade, based both in Jalalabad and Kabul; and the director of the Afghan Reconstruction Group at the U.S. embassy in Kabul. Nangarhar Inc. looked at the province's advantages—an improving security situation, increasing political stability, agricultural potential, and location along a major trade route—and then formed an interagency strategy to use these advantages.

The plan brought together the major U.S. development donors—USAID, CERP, and the State Department's INL specialists (who brought $10 million of "good performance" funds to the province) —and identified economic "enablers" that the Afghans could not provide themselves, such as electricity. Working groups also studied "cold chains"—a network of refrigerated storage facilities for agricultural produce brought to market—as well as farm-to-market roads linking the outlying districts with Jalalabad and the major paved highway. They also looked at how to build a commercial airport in Nangarhar, both to ease business travel and to increase exports.

As a starting point for Nangarhar Inc., the plans section of the 173rd Airborne developed a synchronization matrix of current and proposed projects sponsored by various agencies. This helped clarify who was doing what, where, when, and why. Given the complexity of these endeavors, the initial synchronization matrix coordinated only U.S. projects, but then incorporated Afghan and international development efforts in a later phase.

The COIN aspects of Nangarhar Inc. centered on the expansion of the economy and the creation of jobs. Jobs were particularly important to give alternatives to young men who might otherwise join insurgent groups for employment (rather than ideological) reasons. It was also needed to provide jobs and livelihoods to replace the considerable economic loss some districts suffered by reducing the poppy crop. Economic development, particularly visible signs of progress such as roads, demonstrated that the Afghan government was able to provide a better life to its people. Economic progress also served to justify the presence of Coalition forces in an area traditionally wary of foreigners. It also delivered an asymmetric advantage over insurgent groups that could not provide economic development (and whom the people saw as hindering progress).

The ARG provided expertise on airport development, but more importantly, contacted private investors to bring capital to the province. This was not impossible — the private telecommunications industry in Afghanistan had been a huge success — but the weak legal framework for business, security, and problems over land titles made most investors reluctant.

The 173rd plans section eventually brought its synchronization matrix and future plans section to the U.S. Embassy in Kabul for a ten-day review and polish, and then presented it to the leadership of U.S. embassy and the 101st Airborne Division. It was later shared with the provincial leaders and the wider international community.

Several positive factors made Nangarhar Inc. a viable possibility: improved security, the availability of development funds, emerging local governance, an economic base of agriculture and trade, and the involvement of several U.S. agencies. Clearly, this project could not be replicated in every province of Afghanistan. However, Herat and Balkh provinces (in the northwest), also located on trade routes, might have presented similar opportunities, while Kandahar and Khost provinces had similar opportunities in terms of trade and agriculture — but also had considerable security challenges. Nangarhar Inc. was an asymmetric counterinsurgency tool, in that the Taliban and other insurgent groups could not provide basic infrastructure such as roads, irrigation systems, electrical generation and distribution grids, and civilian airports.

Nangarhar Inc. was a decent first attempt at a difficult task — interagency coordination aimed at the multiple goals of counternarcotics, counterinsurgency, economic development, and the establishment of local governance. Interagency coordination within the U.S. government was made easier since Jalalabad was only thirty to forty minutes by plane from Kabul. Helicopters and fixed-wing planes shuttled embassy officers to JAF for meetings and brought Army officers to the Embassy. High-level support from the U.S. ambassador, the deputy chief of mission, and the leadership of the

101st Airborne Division gave the project a needed push and encouraged civilian agencies to participate. At the same time, efforts by the ARG to attract private investment were important. Given the long timelines for the reconstruction of Afghanistan, complementing international donors with domestic private capital were necessary.

Lessons Learned from the U.S. Engagement in Nangarhar

Because the population was almost entirely Pashtun, counterinsurgency efforts in Nangarhar were more likely to succeed, since there were minimal ethnic clashes. Many people, especially the younger generation, seemed to want to move forward and reject the Taliban's very conservative social policies. The relative quiet during the early years of this period in adjacent agencies of Pakistan's FATA contributed to the successes in Nangarhar. The large Shiite population in adjacent Kurram Agency made it harder for the (Sunni) Taliban to operate across the border in Afghanistan.

At the same time, USG interagency cooperation improved at the embassy in Kabul and at the task force headquarters in Bagram—although this required considerable effort. The proximity of Jalalabad to both Kabul and Bagram facilitated this coordination. In addition, the presence of the large brigade headquarters at JAF provided a visible sign of coalition commitment that seemed to increase the confidence of local leaders, while encouraging the "fence-sitters" to align with the government and giving the population the confidence to reject the Taliban.

The general support from the population for the coalition and the Afghan government, especially the ANA, was critical. While programs to build up Afghan security forces received considerable resources, the civil service side did not benefit from an equivalent effort. At the end of the period under review, there was still a pressing need to strengthen local government at all levels (particularly the civil service cadre), and improve formal justice systems. Improvement of the education system, including teacher training, was also crucial to the sustainment of democracy.

Nangarhar was the political and economic "center of gravity" for this part of Afghanistan, so COIN progress there was relevant to the neighboring provinces of Konar, Laghman, and Nuristan. In addition, positive results in Nangarhar may have positively influenced the adjacent Kurram, Bajaur, and Khyber agencies of the FATA.

Epilogue

During a temporary assignment to Afghanistan in early 2010, I asked U.S. civilian and military officials about the status of Nangarhar Inc. While parts of the plan had been adopted, particularly short-term projects, the overall strategy and long-term planning had been superseded by new initiatives.

By 2011–2012, the security situation in Nangarhar was worsening, and crime was a serious problem, while Governor Shirzai's grip on the province was weakening.[71] By the 2010–2011 growing season, poppy cultivation was increasing in the province, and it was not clear that counter-narcotics efforts were sustainable, particularly in the face of local opposition to CN tactics.[72]

The next chapter will look at some of the fundamental causes of the fighting along the Pakistan- Afghanistan border—in particular—the reaction of a conservative society to rapid modernization, the influx of conservative religious ideas into Pashtun society, and the social fraying due to decades of wars.

Irrigated fields with Spin Ghar mountain range in background, Nangarhar Province.

Jalalabad city center as seen from a helicopter.

Nangarhar Case Study   125

Local Market, Jalalabad city, Nangarhar Province.

Nangarhar Governor Shirzai (center) and Konar Governor Wahidi (right).

11

The Rise of Radical Islam in the Border Areas

The rise of radical Islam along both sides of the Afghan-Pakistan border was rooted in three major factors. The first was the disintegration of Afghan social structures at both the state and tribal levels, beginning in 1979 with revolts against the Communist government and the subsequent Soviet invasion. The second was the increased sway of political Islam, due mostly to outside influences, including Salafist thought from the Middle East and the more local Deobandi philosophy. The third was the radicalization of the Pashtuns, the dominant ethnic group along the border. This chapter will examine how these three converging factors contributed to instability on both sides of the border, and where it might lead.

The Increasing Influence of Radical Islam in Afghanistan

One initial step towards more radical forms of Islam was in the 1970s, when Afghan students returning from Egypt formed an Afghan branch of the Muslim Brotherhood. A much greater influence, however, was the growth of radical mujahedeen groups based in Pakistan during the war against the Soviets.[73] Of the seven major mujahedeen groups, the government of Pakistani President Zia-ul-Haq favored those with more radical leanings, particularly the HIG of Hekmatyar, the Jamaat-e-Islami (Islamic Party) under Rabbani, and the faction under Abdul Rasul Sayyaf (which was also backed by Saudi Arabia). More moderate elements received less money and arms or were forced to merge with the better-supported groups.

Following an Afghan wartime tradition, mullahs stepped forward to become military commanders during the war against the Soviets. Almost certainly, the length and intensity of the war, coupled with the destruction of the Afghan state, increased the role of mullahs in society. At the same time, as the war against the Soviets dragged on, the Afghan education system largely ceased to exist; as a result, madrassas in Pakistan began to provide religion-based education to refugees.

This combination of factors—Pakistani support for mujahedeen factions, the displacement of large numbers of refugees who were then educated in madrassas (and also lost ties with their tribes and communities), and the concept of "jihad" against an atheistic superpower—was a step towards radical Islam gaining influence in Afghanistan. The next major impetus was the rise of the Taliban.

The theology and the philosophy of the Taliban reflects that of the Deobandis, a sect founded in India in 1867. The Deobandis promoted a conservative interpretation of the Koran, rejecting innovations to Sharia law in response to modern factors. They also opposed any hierarchy within the community, excluded Shiites, and restricted the role of women in society. As the Taliban took Kandahar in late 1994 and Kabul in September 1996, they imposed this strict interpretation of Islam on Afghan society, particularly regarding the role of women. These social policies shocked many Afghans who, while being deeply religious—at the same time—did not adhere to the Taliban's extreme views and social mores.

With the return of Osama bin-Laden from Sudan in mid-1996, the conservative Islam of al-Qaeda was added to that of the Taliban. Perhaps more important was the financial and military support provided by al-Qaeda to the Taliban, overlaid with bin-Laden's call for defense of Muslims worldwide and for jihad against the Western world.

Political Islam in Western Pakistan

Because Pakistan was founded, in part, as a homeland for Muslims, the impact of Islam on every facet of society should come as no surprise. However, the last thirty years have seen an increase in the influence of radical Islamist movements in Pakistani society, particularly in the NWFP, (since renamed Khyber Pakhtunhwa) and the FATA bordering Afghanistan. The NWFP also contains much of Pakistan's Pashtun population.

The increasing influence of radical Islamism in the NWFP, in part, parallels the events occurring in Afghanistan—the Soviet invasion, followed by the influx of millions of Afghan refugees into camps, and the Pakistani Government's support of the jihad and mujahedeen groups. Since the 1950s, the border areas had seen a large increase in the number of madrassas, many reportedly funded by Saudi Arabia. Lacking alternatives, many refugee children, as well as poor Pakistanis, attended these madrassas.

Added to this was the rule of General Zia-ul-Haq from 1977 to 1988. The general, a devout Muslim, supported the jihad in Afghanistan while encouraging the Islamization of the economic and legal system in Pakistan, including policies that increased Sunni-Shiite tensions. He also encouraged the growth of the madrassa system. This period also saw a rise in the influence of mullahs and Islamic scholars in society and the increased power of political parties, such as the Jamaat-e-Islami.

Many analysts believe that following the Taliban's fall in 2001, many of the regime's members and supporters fled across the border into Pakistan, particularly into the ethnically Pashtun areas around Peshawar and the FATA. Press reports have also alleged that known Taliban figures took refuge in Quetta, the largest city in Pakistan's Baluchistan province. The Taliban, along with other radical Islamist groups including al-Qaeda, HIG, and the Haqqani network, then attempted to establish themselves and their extremist beliefs in the NWFP.

The Radicalization of the Pashtuns

Although mixed with Tajiks, Peshaei, Baluchs, and Nuristanis, the Pashtuns are by far the predominant ethnic group in the Pakistan-Afghanistan border region. Most Pashtuns share a common language (Pashto) and strict codes of social conduct, based on honor, revenge, hospitality, and the provision of asylum. In physical appearance they vary greatly, from those with pale skin and fair hair to others with black hair and darker features.

For reasons similar to those that have changed other parts of Afghan society, Pashtun society has undergone considerable transformation over the last thirty years, and the degree of radicalization perhaps exceeds that of any other Afghan ethnic group. This may reflect, in part, their heavy involvement, on both sides of the border, in the war against the Soviets. The Taliban, besides being an organization with very conservative religious beliefs, may also be viewed as a Pashtun organization; this connection may have increased the radicalization of society.

The largely Pashtun-based insurgency may also be tied to the rapid imposition of modernity on what is essentially a rural, traditional, clan-based society. Some Pashtuns may see insurgency as a way to fend off the inroads of foreign movies, liberal thought, drugs, and the relaxation of social restraints on women.

The Advent of Suicide Bombings in Afghanistan

During the period 2004–2008, the border areas of Pakistan and Afghanistan saw a new and disturbing phenomenon: the suicide bomber. As a UNAMA paper notes, "Before the assassination of Ahmad Shah Massoud on September 9, 2001, the notion that suicide might be used to kill others was considered alien."[74] Although suicide bombing may have been adapted from tactics used in the war in Iraq, it is worth examining the causes of this phenomenon and its place in border society.

In the spring of 2005, a young Afghan lined up to enter the health clinic at the American-led PRT in Khost Province, along the border with Pakistan. Later dubbed "Lucky," he lacked one arm, and an empty eye socket was badly infected. Guards, noticing his nervous behavior, approached him. The bomber attempted to detonate the bomb and the grenades strapped to his body, failing in both. Detained, he told soldiers his family would be paid thousands of dollars after his mission was complete, and that he felt, given his poor health, he had little to lose.

Later that year, in neighboring Gardez, Paktia Province, security guards allowed a young Afghan to approach Provincial Governor Taniwal's vehicle. When Taniwal opened the car door to speak to the man, the Afghan detonated the bomb on his body, killing the governor. Taniwal, a professional associate of this author and a gentle, professorial man, had returned from exile in Australia to a dangerous and difficult job, in part, out of patriotism.

In conversations with the author, Afghans of various social classes stressed that suicide bombing does not have cultural roots in Afghanistan and that suicide is forbidden under Islam (while often blaming foreigners, particularly Pakistanis, for the attacks). The UNAMA report notes: "The Afghan mujahedeen commanders did not use suicide attacks against the Russians, nor did the Taliban and the Northern Alliance use it against each other.[75] The year 2007 saw more than 140 suicide attacks, with the majority aimed at Afghan and international security forces—along with government officials—although a large number of innocent civilians were also victims.

As noted in the Khost example, some bombers were motivated by financial considerations. Others acted out of religious convictions, acquired in the madrassas that taught not only a strict interpretation of the Koran, but also the necessity of holy war against foreigners and Afghans allied with them. Within this context, the concept of self-sacrifice (*shahadah*) evolved. Taught at a young age, the amalgamation of these ideas drove some young men to view suicide bombing as a noble act of piety. The large numbers of refugees disconnected from their social, tribal, and cultural roots (as well as the Pashtun emulation of the mujahedeen who fought against the Soviets) also contributed to the development of such ways of thinking. Conversations in 2007 and 2008 with U.S. and ISAF military officers suggest a third group of suicide bombers: those who were mentally disturbed or mentally deficient, and were manipulated or deceived into carrying out bombings. A fourth group were those who were unwitting—for example, a taxi driver who had explosives hidden in his car, which are then detonated by remote control.

Suicide Bombing in Pakistan

While the period 2004-2005 was characterized by insurgent groups partially based in Pakistan launching attacks across the border into Afghanistan, by the end of 2007, the insurgents were increasingly aiming at the Pakistani state and security apparatus. One of their tactics was suicide bombing, as rare in Pakistan as it had been in Afghanistan until the twenty-first century. The most high-profile attacks were against former Prime Minister Benazir Bhutto in

Karachi and Rawalpindi, and two separate attacks against then-Interior Minister Aftab Sherpao in April and December 2007. There was also a shift in mid-2006 when, after an airstrike against a madrassa in the Bajaur Agency of the FATA, militants began targeting Pakistani security forces in various parts of Pakistan, including a bloody attack on a Special Forces base in September 2007. Following the July 2007 storming of the Red Mosque held by a group of Islamist militants in Islamabad, militants targeted the Pakistani Inter-Services Intelligence (ISI). In September and again in November 2007, suicide bombers targeted buses carrying ISI personnel. The targeting of Pakistani security organizations represented a shift in the strategy of the militants, who since the war against the Soviets, had largely coexisted with them. Militant Sunni groups, including the Taliban, also targeted Shiites in the FATA, particularly in the Kurram Agency. Fighting that began in December 2007 resulted in a considerable influx of Shiites into Khost and Paktia provinces in Afghanistan.

Madrassas and the Education System

The years of war caused considerable damage to Afghanistan's education system, particularly in the rural areas. The Taliban regime made the situation worse through a combination of inept administration, a focus on religious education to the exclusion of secular subjects, and a policy of denying education to girls. By the time the Taliban was overthrown, primary education had nearly ceased to exist in some areas. Some Pashtun areas, such as Paktika Province, had almost no functioning schools. The first development priorities for many people in the province were not roads, power, or health clinics, but schools. Coalition forces made a concerted effort to refurbish existing school houses and construct new schools, but reviving the system will take years due to lack of trained teachers, administrators, and money to pay them. As a result, many parents started sending their children to madrassas, including those across the border in Pakistan, to receive at least some education.

While the Afghan government and the international community made real progress in rebuilding the state education system, there were also efforts underway to build a more moderate system of madrassa education. In a January 12, 2008 interview with the

BBC, Education Minister Dr. Hanif Atmar said, "We are critical of policies in the past. Actually it was a result of those policies to exclude these madrassas, keep them on the margin of the society, and then entirely hand them over to the fundamentalists." He added, "In Pakistan across the border with Afghanistan there are around 15,000 madrassas, and around 1.5 million students are enrolled there. If we invest adequately, and according to the policy of the government of Afghanistan, in our madrassa system, to a large extent those Afghans who are now being taught in madrassas across the border will come back to their own country." In the same interview, the Speaker of the Upper House of the Afghan parliament, Sibghatullah Mujadidi, said, "In Pakistan some of our students are studying religious subjects and they have been also trained for terrorism. If we have enough madrassas in Afghanistan, there will be no need for students to go to Pakistan. They will study here and real moderate Islam will be taught to them."[76]

The Future of Religious Extremism in the Border Areas

The Pashtuns, progressively radicalized as a result of the confluence of social dislocation, war, outside extremist influences, and a radicalized religious educational system, have been caught in trends beyond their control. At the same time, they were willing participants in a religious and patriotic war against the Soviets, and many joined the Taliban in its campaigns against secular influences and the other ethnic groups of Afghanistan in the1990s. The Pashtuns were increasingly aligned against the Pakistani state, as shown by the attacks on the ISI and the Pakistani military in 2007.

Conversations with Afghans in 2007 and 2008 often showed a general rejection of both continued war and religious extremism. While Afghanistan is a nation with a remarkable, deeply ingrained religion, the strictures of the Taliban particularly those of the Ministry of Enforcement of Virtue and Suppression of Vice, were out of step with much of Afghan society. In the Pashtun areas, the existing code of "pakhtunwali" based on honor, revenge, and hospitality, made it difficult for Sharia law to gain a firm foothold. After being subjected to wide swings of political systems—royalist, communist, anarchy, theocracy, then a veneer of democracy (underlain by a strong grassroots democracy, demonstrated by the "shura" system of community consultations) — many people seemed to desire normalcy, with economic, political, and social stability and progress.

Pakistan has been caught off guard by the blowback from their support for the Taliban and the more radical mujahedeen groups during the 1980s, with resulting instability in the Pashtun areas of the NWFP. Faced with this threat, the Pakistani military began, with U.S. aid, to adopt a counterinsurgency strategy similar to that underway in Afghanistan, based on enhancing the capability of local security forces, improving economic opportunities, and improving governance in the Tribal Areas.

In 2006 the Pakistani government conducted a systematic review of its policies in the FATA and concluded that, like insurgencies in Afghanistan and Iraq, theirs could not be solved by military means alone. In close consultation with tribal elders from all seven agencies of the FATA, the Pakistani government developed a nine-year, $2 billion Sustainable Development Plan designed to extend its writ over un-governed spaces within its sovereign borders. The U.S. pledged to support this development plan with $750 million over five years. The U.S. also began training, equipping, and expanding the ethnically Pashtun Frontier Corps—the only viable local security force that can defend local towns against militant and extremist infiltration.

The current insurgency in Afghanistan and Pakistan had complex local roots beyond the ideological and geopolitical factors outlined in this chapter, including more mundane issues such as poverty, unemployment, poor education, and ethnic differences. At the same time, the deep cultural traditions of the border areas (particularly the role of women in society) were colliding daily with the modern world. Radio, television, the internet, cell phones, DVDs, new roads, and returning refugees were bringing new ideas and new customs to what had been a very conservative, traditional, somewhat homogenous culture. This may have reflected the struggle ongoing within the larger world of Islam, as values and beliefs clashed with an increasingly global culture and morality. The people of the border areas will eventually decide for themselves how to proceed, in spite of outside influences pushing more radical forms of Islam. This will be a long process, taking decades, and one the Western world has only a limited ability to alter.

12

Analysis of the U.S. Engagement in RC-East

This chapter will analyze how successful the U.S.-led intervention in eastern Afghanistan was. First, were the strategies and tactics appropriate to the general goals of stability, a credible, functioning Afghan government, and the ability of that government to provide security and defend its borders? How were strategies and tactics adjusted over time? Were the goals the correct ones, in the end? How much did U.S., Afghan and Pakistani goals differ? What were the metrics used to measure progress? Second, did these efforts prepare the ground for the next period of intervention, beginning in 2009 with the increased troop and financial resources brought to bear, along with an increased focus on population security?

Security

The presence of U.S. and ISAF military forces in RC-East during this period was important for multiple reasons. First, they gave the ANSF enough time to recruit, train, and deploy to border areas, beginning in significant numbers by 2004 and 2005. Once the Afghan units began to deploy, U.S. forces worked with them as mentors and in joint operations, increasing their confidence and capabilities, particularly in operations involving larger units and more complex operational planning. Second, the military presence along the border areas of RC-East served as a shield from insurgents aiming at Kabul, the political center of gravity—even though small groups could still get through. Third, these forces gave a degree of confidence to the local population that felt threatened by the insurgents and other armed groups, and provided some protection to local government centers as these gradually expanded their reach. Importantly for U.S. security strategy, including homeland security, al-Qaeda was largely unable to operate in RC-East in any major, strategically significant way. In a sense, RC-East was a successful holding action while operations in Iraq took precedence— maintaining a presence while doing what needed to be done to maintain stability, and establishing a foundation for the surge of troops and civilians that began in 2009.

Considerable effort was put into targeting and fighting insurgent groups and eliminating individual terrorist leaders. At times this seemed to take on a momentum of its own, beyond or apart from securing the population as required by the COIN strategy. This may have reflected some unit's preference for taking the fight directly to those it perceived as the enemy. Also, the priority put on either the CT mission or the COIN missions by top leadership was different in different years, resulting in more direct action in some periods.

The US military presence, coupled with the ANSF once it began to deploy in significant numbers, certainly hindered insurgent efforts. Arguably, this foreign presence may have also given the insurgents and jihadists a rallying point. However, the insurgency would have occurred regardless, as the Taliban, the Haqqani Network, HIG and other groups sought to assert control over parts of Afghanistan and weaken the Karzai government.

Reconciliation programs aimed at insurgents groups, such as the Takhim-e-Solh Program (PTS) during this period were not very effective in –RC-East. In the author's experience, they were underfunded, and lacked sufficient manpower and organizational structure. More importantly, they did not make adequate provisions for jobs and security for insurgents who chose to reconcile. By 2009, these shortfalls were clear, both in terms of the limited numbers of reconciled fighters relative to the overall numbers of fighters, and the lack of a solid program to build on.

Development and Reconstruction

During this period, several hundred million dollars of development assistance of various types flowed into RC-East. Certainly there was a need—this was a very poor area, and there was little private investment, with the exception of telecommunications. This large infusion of funds clearly supported COIN efforts at the tactical level by supporting military operations and the nascent GOA, Some of these development programs, including CERP, showed some degree of success. During the earlier years of this period, most CERP projects were relatively small, including building or refurbishing of schools, health clinics, markets, irrigation systems, and the upgrading of existing roads. By 2007, large amounts of funding were being channeled through CERP, with some PRTs handling tens of millions of dollars—a major shift in COIN efforts, and how the United States carried out development. In the end, it was hard to determine how much impact this investment may have had, either in terms of development or COIN.

Government

Governance improved in RC-East during this time, starting from a very low initial baseline. By 2009 a foundation of provincial-level government was in place, including some good governors. Elections had been held for provincial councils, Afghans were becoming more accustomed to voting and representative government, and more attention and resources were going to district-level government. However, these gains were still reversible, and uneven from place to place. A clear weakness by 2009 was the lack of a large enough civil service cadre, and sufficient local training and mentoring programs to produce more of them. This was in sharp contrast to training levels of the ANA and later the ANP, both of which eventually received considerable support.

Rule of Law

The Rule of Law (ROL) program in RC-East, intended to develop the justice sector, did not show enough progress to set a solid foundation for later efforts. The justice sector was a daunting problem—initial institutional baselines were very low; developing the necessary human resources required considerable time; there were competing national priorities for the lawyers, prosecutors, and judges that did exist; while there were competing versions of local law. After the initial Bonn conference, Italy was designated as the lead-nation for ROL for all of Afghanistan, but did not put much effort into RC-East; this was time lost that was hard to regain once the insurgency gained momentum. Subsequent Afghan and USG efforts up to 2008 were under-resourced and disjointed. Weakness in the judicial sector held back the formal business sector, made successful prosecution of government officials for corruption almost nonexistent at the provincial level, made overlapping land claims difficult to resolve, and gave the Taliban a "wedge" to expand its influence by providing its version of justice. In hindsight, ROL should have been given more emphasis from the beginning, with a long-term program to build up the formal sector, and perhaps a short-term program to support the informal justice sector. For example, legal academies, concurrent with public administration schools, could have been established in the major RC-East towns such as Jalalabad and Ghazni.

Corruption as a Fundamental Problem

Corruption was clearly a problem in RC-East during this period, but was generally dealt with in an ad-hoc basis, if at all. This was a difficult issue for the Coalition—clear proof of corruption was rare, and it was often necessary to work with officials despite strong suspicions. Even with pro0of, the justice system could not adequately address the problem, and the will from Kabul to deal with the issue often seemed lacking. There were strong cultural underpinnings, including patronage systems, extended families that expected support from relatives with money or influence, and the fact that corruption had already been in place for decades, or longer. Some weak GOA systems, including antiquated accounting methods and gaps in oversight, increased opportunities for corruption. Some Afghans were hoarding money as a hedge against future chaos in the country, while at the same time relatively large amounts of drug money were injected into the economy, increasing corruption (although less so in RC-East, relative to RC-South). All of these factors made it difficult for foreigners to make a sustained, positive impact against corruption.

An Accidental Fight with the Pashtuns?

In RC-East the Coalition may have backed into some conflicts unnecessarily. The potential causes for these conflicts were plentiful, but were often related to a poor understanding of local conditions, cultural factors, or pre-existing tribal issues. The use of military force at times had unintended consequences, including the reciprocal use of force by locals. Coalition officers at times inadvertently backed one side in a preexisting struggle, thereby alienating the other party. Examples include friction with the Waziri tribe in Paktika Province when some units backed the Kharotis, despite a longstanding enmity between the two groups. The friction with the Korangalis in Konar and Nuristan was more complex, and among U.S. officers there was a wide variety of views of what fueled it. Some attributed it to a general dislike of outsiders by the Korangalis; others, to their being co-opted by foreign fighters; and still others, to the disruption of their timber smuggling businesses. Conflict with the Zadran tribe in the area where Khost, Paktika and Paktia provinces intersect was similarly complex, driven by ties with the Haqqanis (who were largely Zadran), questions of economic and political influence, and resistance to outside influences that might change their conservative society.

In a larger sense, the Pashtuns and the United States may have backed into unnecessary friction and conflict. Initial misunderstandings by the local population over what the U.S. intent and goals were in RC-East was one factor. This was coupled with the Taliban, other insurgent groups, and outside actors operating within Pashtun society, while also trying to mobilize this society against the United States. Some of this friction may have been inevitable—the high value Pashtuns put on honor and revenge make intervention by any foreign force fraught with pitfalls. Once the shooting started, including sweeps by maneuver units and the use of night raids and attack aircraft, unintended casualties and incidents were very difficult to completely avoid. Because the ANA did not have sufficient capacity to deploy early in this period, the United States largely lacked the cultural and social insights which they could have provided, and it was harder to put an "Afghan face" on operations. In retrospect it would have been useful if the Afghan government had organized a Pashtun *loya jirga*—a conference of tribal elders—to discuss the foreign troop deployment along the border in 2004, if not earlier, as well as earlier cross-border "peace jirgas." Local buy-in by such a jirga to a U.S. presence could have made a considerable difference. On the other hand, Tajiks, Hazaras and much of the Pashtun population in RC-East seemed supportive of the international presence. While many company-level and Special Forces units did a good job of working at the local level, closer to the population, greater numbers of small units living and working among the population would have helped avoid unnecessary clashes between the Pashtuns and foreign forces.

There was a gradual drift into insurgency/counterinsurgency during this time, which became sharper and escalated in many areas by early 2005. This reflected the additional resources available to insurgent groups, including the establishment and expansion of sanctuaries that, by making the insurgency more viable, made it more inevitable. The historic tendency towards armed conflict in the border areas made it easier to touch off an insurgency. Also, the many factions became more entrenched as the fighting went on, making it more difficult to arrive at a political solution, which in the end may have been the only way to end the conflict.

Avoidable Fights with the NGOs?

Some NGO workers argued that the presence of the U.S. military was the major factor fueling the conflict, in the sense their presence caused the Pashtuns to organize a resistance. This is unlikely—the Taliban would have tried to reestablish themselves in Afghanistan regardless, as would the Haqqani network and HIG. Tensions between NGOs and the military were inevitable, in part, due to differences over who had precedence in the so-called "humanitarian space," and, in part, due to misunderstandings that can develop between those from two very different cultures. This could have been dealt with better by organizing more coordinating conferences early in this period, and efforts at liaison by both sides.

Border Issues as a Key Determinant for COIN

As documented in chapter 9, the long border with Pakistan was of fundamental importance both at the tactical level (roughly within

100 miles of the border), and at a strategic level throughout RC-East, north to Kabul. Considerable effort went into coordinating with Pakistani security forces, which established a foundation for later cooperation and coordination, although more effort could have been put into coordinating with Pakistani political actors in the NWFP. There were initial misunderstandings by the United States of the limited capabilities of some of the Pakistani forces along the border, and their willingness to fight against insurgents. The mix of forces between regular Pakistani military, Frontier Corps, kassadars, and militias made the situation complex and subject to change. The situation in Afghanistan was hard enough to understand; coalition officers did not always have the time, or sources of information, to focus on the other side of the border.

The initial misjudgment by U.S. officers of the goals and strategies of actors in Pakistan had significant implications. While U.S. and Afghan field-grade officers (particularly Special Forces) were clear that attacks were being organized and launched by insurgents from the other side of the border, it was not apparent at first how much of this was part of a larger strategy of either acceptance, or assistance, by some actors. The handling of border issues and the understanding of related insurgencies occurring in two countries was made harder by the lack of deep coordination and communication between the embassies in Kabul and Islamabad, along with the consulate in Peshawar, during the early part of this period

Brussels and New York as Factors

Preexisting situations in Brussels had an impact in Afghanistan. Cooperation between NATO and the EU was held back, in part, by blocks over Cypriot, Greek, and Turkish issues. This became more important in RC-East once Polish, French and Czech forces became engaged there, and could not draw on EU resources. At the same time, some argued that COIN was outside of NATO's core competencies.

While UNAMA officers were often talented and knowledgeable, they were limited in numbers and lacked adequate resources. Given the complexity of the situation on the ground—and the amount of money and effort being expended—having more of these officers would have been money well spent, particularly as they were seen as neutral players by most Afghans.

A positive outcome of the U.S. and international presence was that it raised expectations among Afghans that a better civil society was both attainable and deserved, after decades of war. The elections of 2004 and 2005, the large influx of various types of assistance, and programs to build up government and the justice system contributed to these expectations. Similarly, the international presence encouraged and helped a new generation of Afghan leaders to emerge, including governors and mayors who will become national leaders. Imperfect as progress was in some areas of civil society, the effects will make it much harder for the Taliban to return, given their unpopularity among Afghans, particularly Afghan women, and their poor record of running the country.

Analysis of Alternative Strategies

Given the rugged terrain, the logistical difficulties of operating in eastern Afghanistan, and the vulnerability of small bases to attacks by concentrations of insurgents, some argued for focusing efforts mostly on lines of communications (LOCs)—usually major roads and highways—and population centers. In the late 1980s, the Soviets eventually defaulted to this approach, in part because of the strong insurgency in the area later covered by RC-East. However, during the period 2004–2008, covering the rural areas deemed critical for COIN as well as the LOCs and population centers made sense. This strategy prevented the establishment of large insurgent safe havens in Afghanistan, helped protect Kabul and other cities, and gave more confidence to "fencesitters" in rural areas. It was also *possible*, given the U.S. Army's excellent logistical capability, and the new or improved roads that were constructed. The smaller bases also helped protect the provincial capitals, and gave the local government more breathing room as they became established. In a more general sense, Afghans wanted their country to become a consolidated and viable state, and extending control to as many areas as practicable made this more likely.

An alternative, or complementary, approach would have been to pay off the tribes to support the Karzai government and the

Coalition and oppose the Taliban. There was a precedent for this approach—the British used it along the border between India and Afghanistan during the Raj, with some success. Development projects may have achieved something similar by channeling money in ways that favored some tribes. Given the high costs of deploying U.S. military forces, it may have been more cost-efficient to pay the tribes off. However, this would not have been best for Afghan society in the long-run, as it would have strengthened these tribes relative to the government and security services.

Differing Views on the Roles of Local Militias

An important security debate during this period was over establishing or maintaining existing local militias to help secure the local population. Although by 2005 most local militias had been demobilized, by 2008 this idea was being reconsidered by the United States. There were strong arguments against this step. First was that idea that limited resources should instead go to the ANA and ANP. Second was the potential difficulty of controlling these militias, and the possibility they could end up attacking other militias, turning to organized crime, or attacking the government and Coalition forces (or a mix of these). The arguments in favor were that they would give communities the means to defend themselves against insurgents, provide a local presence while the ANSF was being built up, and be relatively low-cost in comparison to military units. By 2010 the argument in favor of local militias won out, with the establishment of the Afghan Local Police program, despite reluctance on the part of the Karzai administration and Ambassador Eikenberry.[77]

Despite the conflicts of the previous thirty years, society in this part of Afghanistan retained its resilience, through the strength of traditional social structures, Islam, family and clans. The years after the fall of the Taliban until the insurgency gained momentum five year later gave this society a chance to regroup, and it will hold together in the long term.[78]

Metrics — Determining the Success or Failure of COIN

Determining which metrics were relevant, collecting and analyzing this information, and then applying it to determine or modify strategy was crucial. None of these steps were easy, given the situation, or as well done as they could have been. In the earlier years of this period, much of the data collected was numerical—the number of schools built or the number of troops in contact, for example—and less geared towards any narrative that put these numbers into a wider context, or reflected what locals thought the future might bring. Numerical data, while easier to present, (particularly in powerpoint slides, the preferred means of briefings at FOBs, PRTs and Bagram) also had the disadvantage of not necessarily reflecting impact. For example, the numbers of schools built might not reflect either learning by students, or increased capacity in the Ministry of Education. Also, these numbers were fed upwards into a large system where higher-level analysts and consumers may or may not have had enough context to interpret them correctly.

To their credit, civilians in the PRTs did some excellent reporting that integrated different economic, security, governance, and social factors into cables (frequently drawing on the impressions of soldiers), and military officers often fed insightful analysis to their higher commands. By 2008 the Coalition had a better understanding of the overall situation, in part, due to accumulated experience, in part, due to better collection, such as that by "Human Terrain Teams" composed of anthropologists. Some of the best publicly available information on Afghan's views were the yearly Asia Foundation surveys.

Some of the most important metrics were the hardest to gauge. For example, the effectiveness of local government, and the population's support for their government were both fundamental for the COIN campaign, but hard to collect and quantify. Local polling data was almost nonexistent during this time, so that, beyond anecdotal evidence, it was difficult to objectively judge how individual governors or mayors were doing—and since they were appointed rather than elected, voter sentiment was not available as an indicator. Long-term trends were also difficult to measure, since data collection was not always systematic over time, and frequent unit rotations hindered continuity. The increased insurgent activity beginning in 2005 made an accurate assessment of the situation harder, as security constraints put more distance between international officers and the Afghan population.

Other measurements could have provided relevant metrics. For example, data on the numbers of Afghans returning to or permanently departing the country, and moving from insecure areas of the countryside into the (relatively safer) cities could have given a sense of security trends, and of Afghan's judgment of their future prospects. Similarly, money flowing out of Afghanistan into overseas banks, relative to direct foreign investment, would have been relevant.

While provincial governors usually had a good understanding of the local situation, the GOA in Kabul was not as well-informed about events outside of the capitol, particularly in the earlier days of this period. As communications, particularly e-mail and cellphone coverage began to expand, this improved. Eventually, IDLG required that governors send regular reports to Kabul, while the National Directorate for Security initiated reporting, although these provided only two perspectives on the situation.[79]

Conclusions on the U.S. Engagement in RC-East from 2004 to 2008

Building up the local governance structure, bolstering the economy and infrastructure, and expanding the reach of the ANSF—while fighting an active insurgency—were tremendously difficult undertakings, and the odds were not favorable in 2004. Any one of these tasks would have been hard. Against that yardstick, RC-East did well in the three main areas of security, governance, and development, as well as counternarcotics. However, progress was not what was hoped for in early days, and certainly did not reach what could have been achieved in a best-case scenario. Much of this was due to security problems—fighting an insurgency and other "bad actors" took up a huge percentage of time and resources. The presence of insurgent sanctuaries across the border in Pakistan made a clear COIN "win" in RC-East extremely difficult to achieve, particularly given the porosity of this border. By 2008 there was a stalemate of sorts, with neither side able to prevail.

The insurgents could (and did) claim successes in RC-East during this time. It was certainly easier for them to destabilize the nascent Afghan government than for the government to govern and pacify the provinces. It was much easier for the insurgents to carry out point attacks, bombings, or assassinations than for the government to protect itself and the population. As the number of attacks on coalition forces mounted, the insurgents succeeded in separating the Coalition from the population, as more and more security measures—including heavily armored convoys—were put in place. A particularly pernicious and effective tactic was infiltrating the ANSF, which led to distrust between embedded trainers and mentors on the one hand, and Afghan soldiers and police on the other. If an insurgency wins by virtue of not losing and remaining a viable force, then by this yardstick the Taliban and other insurgents had some success. However, the Afghan population during this time did not provide widespread support for the Taliban—the insurgent's interpretation of Islam, along with their Kandahar origins, did not appeal to Pashtuns in the east (let alone Tajiks or Hazaras), while people were tired of violence and war. The Taliban also had a very poor record of governing during the 1990s. At the same time, the Taliban's tactics and ideology maintained their pariah status among much of the international community.

The struggle along the border was a battle of exhaustion, instead of a battle of attrition or one of decisive battles. The U.S. presence contributed to wearing down the insurgents, turning it into a long and grinding effort—which increased the chances for negotiations and a political solution. At the same time, the insurgents targeted western public opinion, judging the Western publics would tire of a protracted war being waged far away with limited relevance to their daily lives—probably a correct strategy on the part of the insurgents. The insurgents could keep fighting for a long time, particularly given their steady financial and material support, either through state or other actors, narcotics, or criminal activity.

Analysis of RC-East 147

Joint U.S. Army–Afghan National Army patrol, Andar District, Ghazni Province, 2005.

13

Conceptual and Strategic Considerations in RC-East

Several conceptual and strategic factors played a role in RC-East, and to some extent in Afghanistan as a whole. Of considerable importance were international relations, particularly with neighboring countries, which to some extent will determine the fate of Afghanistan. Other important issues were the different concepts of time, the importance (or unimportance) of street demonstrations; government and economics, and the strategic importance of the border regions and Afghanistan to the U.S.

International Aspects

Afghanistan's relations with neighboring countries are complex, and have deep historical roots. Pakistan had by far the most influence over events in RC-East during this period, but it is worth noting the positions of other countries such as Iran, Saudi Arabia, India, and the United Arab Emirates (UAE).

RC-East and the adjacent areas of Pakistan were "welded" together—made inseparable by shared culture, history, trade routes, and language. Pakistan had the most at stake—another Afghan civil war could spill across their borders, igniting their Pashtun population and other dissatisfied groups. Trade with Central Asia was an important consideration for the Pakistani government. This had direct relevance for RC-East, since a major trade route ran through the Khyber Pass, with a lesser route through Khost and Gardez. For this reason alone, the Pakistanis had an interest in a stable Afghanistan.

Pakistan's primary goal was to have a government in Kabul that, at a minimum, was not hostile or, at best, that was aligned with Islamabad. The Pakistanis were very sensitive about Indian presence and activities in Afghanistan, and feared an "envelopment" from both east and west. They maintained the concept of "strategic depth," whereby Afghan territory would aid their defense in the case of an attack on their eastern border. The legal status of the border was an issue, with Afghanistan not formally acknowledging the Duran line, and Pakistan opposed to any talk of a readjustment. However, day-to-day in RC-East this legal issue was far in the background.

During this period, Pakistan closed several refugee camps, with the result that tens of thousands of Afghans crossed the border, often on short notice. In practical terms, the refugee population in Pakistan was one of the most important bilateral issues during this time; the hospitality of the GOP and the Pakistani population was wearing thin, and there was the perception these refugees took some Pakistani jobs; at the same time, the refugee camps were seen as recruiting grounds for insurgent groups.

India reopened its consulate in Jalalabad in late 2002, although it did not seem particularly active. The main Indian interests in RC-East were trade, and the Hajigak iron ore deposit in Bamian, the largest untapped iron deposit in the region. In a more general sense, the Indians wanted a stable Afghanistan that did not provide a base for terrorist operations that could be used against them.

The Iranian Government had previously supported the Shiite Hazara ethnic group (who live in Bamian province, as well as parts of Ghazni), and had cultural and linguistic ties to the Dari-speaking Tajiks as well. Iranian activities during this period were low profile in RC-East, and did not have much, if any, impact on U.S. operations. Afghan officials noted the Iranians were interested in establishing a consulate in Jalalabad, but this never came to fruition.[80]

Saudi Arabia had historically been engaged in the border areas, backing the mujahedeen during the fight against the Soviets, and supporting religious schools. Saudi strategy revolved around its religious agenda, as well as cooperating with Pakistan in some areas, and countering Iranian (Shiite) influence in Afghanistan. During the period 2004–2008, there was little overt Saudi activity in RC-

East. They reportedly began discussions with the Taliban in 2008 at the request of the GOA.

The UAE had development programs in RC-East, including the construction of a large university compound just west of Khost city. In addition, the UAE maintained a small military presence. Khost and the UAE had strong ties, partly as a result of the many Afghan guest workers over the years.

Central Asian countries had several shared concerns, including instability in Afghanistan spilling across their borders; narcotics either being trafficked through their countries, or used by their people; and the potential of Afghanistan becoming a base for radical Islam which could destabilize their countries. On the positive side, they viewed Afghanistan as an important link in trade and transit routes, and Afghans as consumers of electricity and natural gas. While events in RC-East could have an impact on all of these issues, in practical terms the Central Asian countries had no direct impact in RC-East during this time.

Two Different Perspectives

An Afghan Ambassador's Views

In a January 2012 interview by the author, former Afghan Ambassador to the United States Said Jawad noted that Afghan society is changing rapidly,[81] and is much different than the society the United States encountered in 2001. In particular, improvements in education and the rapid spread of internet access are making a considerable difference. However, the degree of change varies considerably within Afghanistan, with parts of the south lagging, and Herat modernizing quickly relative to the rest of Afghanistan. He believes Afghans themselves may not understand fully their own country, given the rapid change of the last ten years.

CFC–A Commander's Views

During an interview by the author in the fall of 2011 in Washington DC, a former CFC-A commander said that tactics and strategies in Afghanistan were largely ad-hoc in the initial years, and that even by 2004, the United States was often "making things up as it went along," and was not fully prepared in terms of strategy or doctrine. In part, this may have reflected that the initial USG intent was to not have a long-term presence in Afghanistan. Washington also made it clear that Afghanistan was an "economy of force operation" while the war in Iraq was being fought.

He noted during this period the interagency was still finding its way—this was "a first date for State and the military." It may have also been an initial mistake by State to "normalize" embassy Kabul, given the circumstances; a different, more unique model may be needed for cases like Afghanistan.[82] While this initial "normalization" may have made civil-military (civ-mil) cooperation more difficult for the military, by 2009 this relationship was working better.[83] At the same time, he said, the lack of Afghan human capital was a significant bottleneck.

A critical question was if the USG was a "learning organization" during these years. In his view, this was ambiguous, since by "2009 people were still acting like people did in the first years of the war." The rapid turnover of ambassadors and top military commanders during this period resulted in a lack of continuity, while military officers at all levels were not kept in place long enough. Instead, there was a tendency to "race for twelve months, then hand the baton off to next guy," rather than focusing on long-term victory. This turnover in personnel and strategies also caused confusion among Afghan counterparts. Rotating the same military units in and out, and keeping the same high-level civil and military staff in place for extended periods would have been the best course of action (although lower-level staff was not as important).

Concepts of Time and Counterinsurgency

Concepts of time in RC-East could not be quantified, but were key. The U.S. military maintained a fast pace, geared to tangible results, usually within one rotation. The Afghans, particularly in rural areas, were on a much slower agrarian clock. The insurgents to some extent saw time as an ally—the phrase "you have the watches, but we have the time" was indicative of their view of the staying power of Coalition forces. The Afghan government, both formal and informal, was often slow-moving and consensual rather than results-oriented and quick. In a more abstract sense, several centuries were present at once, with some rural areas little changed from two hundred years ago. Parts of the Afghan population and the insurgents were from a very tribal, conservative, agrarian society strongly tied to traditional customs. Juxtaposed against this was some very high-tech equipment such as Blackhawks, drones and night-vision goggles. While this technology gave the Coalition considerable tactical advantages, adapting to the nature of Afghan society was the key to any successful COIN strategy—which argues for a long-term, low-tech engagement.

Another variable that cannot be readily quantified is *will*, in the sense of who wants victory (however defined) more. Certainly, the USG cannot want to win a counterinsurgency more than their Afghan allies. This is particularly apparent in levels of corruption, particularly among elites, although the ANA certainly seemed willing to fight. The Afghan population, understandably, is focused more on survival rather than COIN success.

While the current insurgency may eventually burn itself out, it is equally likely to morph into something different, driven by variables and conditions that are currently present. These include regional players using Afghanistan as a battleground for proxy wars, or similarly as an ideological battleground; fighting to control economic factors, particularly revenue streams from drug production and smuggling; ethnic friction; and political power struggles among Afghans and Pakistanis. The increasing urbanization of Afghanistan, with cities such as Kabul, Jalalabad, and Herat doubling or tripling in size in the last ten years may also change the nature of the insurgency, from more rural-based to urban insurgencies.

Significance of Street Demonstrations

Violent demonstrations have occurred in various periods of Afghanistan's history. In RC-East they occurred in Nangarhar in the spring of 2005, and in Kabul and elsewhere after a May 2006 traffic accident involving an ISAF truck. Events like this will need to be managed and prevented as well as possible. Interestingly, perceived affronts to Islam were much more significant than loss of life due to Coalition actions. A combination of factors exacerbated this friction between very different eastern and western cultures. The tendency within Afghan society to believe conspiracies theories and rumors, and the actions of agent provocateurs who turned small, localized events into nationwide demonstrations made this challenging. While these demonstrations eventually passed, there may be a tipping point where Afghan society at large turns against a foreign presence in their country. Until then, Afghan concerns over the actions of neighboring countries, fears of internal social fault lines that could lead to civil war, and the clear need for more international development assistance will counteract those who want the foreigners to leave. This is an argument for reduced foreign troop numbers (while keeping civilian numbers constant), and providing more pre-deployment training for newly assigned officers and those on repeat assignments. It also argues for more reporting on social, cultural, and economic issues to understand shifts in moods, and what tensions and undercurrents might be building in Afghan society. One unintended outcome might be that, with fewer foreigners left in the country, demonstrations would focus more on the Karzai administration, or on his successors after the 2014 elections.

Government and Economics

The legitimacy of the national government is key not only to COIN (including any future GOA campaigns against the insurgents) but also to Afghanistan's future in general. As much as the 2004 presidential elections brought a degree of legitimacy to the GOA and the concept of elections, the allegations of fraud in the 2009 elections had the opposite effect. The irregularities in the 2009 elections may also provide an argument within the Taliban against participating in future elections—if they were ever considering it. Separately, a potential benefit of a substantially reduced U.S. military, aid, and political presence is that it could counter insurgent claims that Karzai and future Afghan governments are puppets of foreigners.

Despite large amounts of international assistance, Afghanistan remains a deeply impoverished country that truly needs a sustained (if ultimately reduced) flow of development support. Even relatively small amounts of money, well-managed and targeted, can make a difference in many Afghan's lives. For example, agricultural assistance is applicable to much of population, is inexpensive relative to large infrastructure programs, has CN and COIN applications, and lends itself to rural stability. The Agricultural Development Teams program was successful and lent itself to areas with poor security. USDA, while it was understaffed and underfunded in Afghanistan, could expand its presence.

Efforts to build up Afghanistan's road and rail infrastructure, coupled with improved rule of law, should eventually help the commercial sector. The transit of goods to central and south Asia, particularly electricity and gas, and remittances from the Persian Gulf will bring money to Afghanistan. Eventually economic interests will prevail, and if the economic benefits are sufficiently widespread, they will take the wind out of the insurgency. On the other hand, any rapid economic development could be destabilizing to what is still, in many parts, a conservative, rural society although, given the hurdles to development, this is unlikely to be a problem anytime soon. On a macroeconomic level a precipitous withdrawal of development funds and military presence from Afghanistan could be disastrous for much of the Afghan population, as described in a recent World Bank study of the Afghan economy.[84]

Strategic Importance to the United States

The strategic importance of –RC-East for the United States—the reasons to continue with a long-term commitment—have faded some with the weakening of al-Qaeda in southwest Asia. However, an ongoing western presence in the border regions of Afghanistan has the advantage of maintaining a presence in an unstable, nuclear-armed region, and providing a buttress against instability spreading either north or south; moreover, a U.S. leadership role is important to future international efforts. While the UN certainly has an important role to play, the U.S. can provide diplomatic, security, and development heft to encourage other countries and organizations to remain engaged for the long term. At the same time, maintaining a presence would negate any perceptions that NATO or the west had lost a war in Afghanistan.

There is a strong moral dimension to the U.S. engagement in

RC-East as well. After a long relationship with Afghanistan, starting in the 1950s with U.S. development assistance, continuing through the fight against the Soviets, and on to the current struggle against Islamic fundamentalists and outside actors, the two nations have been joined in peace and war. This argues for an ongoing American presence until Afghanistan mends from its decades of war. A significant reduction in the U.S. presence may reverse gains in human rights made over the last ten years, particularly for Afghan women and girls, and minorities. The already fragile gains in rule of law, a key to modernizing and stabilizing the country, would also suffer.

The United States—Pakistan relationship historically has strong ups and downs, as the countries' individual interests converge and diverge, with specific incidents such as nuclear smuggling causing friction. The idea that both countries need periodic "cooling off" periods makes sense. While Afghanistan's population, economy and global influence are clearly less than Pakistan's, it is still a Muslim country that is strategically situated, with population that somewhat favors the United States. This argues for maintaining strong ties with Kabul—which, given the difficulty Kabul has with its neighbors, would also be in its interests.

In most cases, foreign intervention can only change societies on the margins, and this was certainly the case in RC-East during this time. While the deployment of considerable U.S. troops and money certainly had an impact on local society, its Pashtun characteristics, in particular, were so deeply rooted and inherent that these changes were not fundamental in their nature. Roads, electricity, education, and telecommunications are changing the border areas, as are the return of expatriate Afghans who have been exposed to different societies. Many young Afghans have more progressive views than their elders—in fact, the reaction to change by the very conservative parts of local society is one of the root causes of the insurgency—one that will burn out over time. What is important for the international community over the long term is to recognize societal shifts, and adjust policies and programs accordingly to increase the chances of success, be it in COIN, development or stabilization operations.

Ending Note

The international engagement during the period 2004–2008 brought a large number of dedicated, courageous officers, soldiers, and development workers to eastern Afghanistan, and presented them with a daunting set of challenges. In hindsight, their efforts to hold together a situation that could easily have spun off into a chaotic mess were admirable. Clearly, more progress could have been made, but the impediments to progress, some very deep-seated and present long before 2004, make the actual progress accomplished remarkable. For the sake of these officers and soldiers, and the many innocent Afghans caught up in the repeated cycles of violence and insecurity, their efforts should not have been made in vain.

Review of Afghan National Army troops by U.S. National Security Advisor Stephen Hadley, Paktia Province, 2005.

Annexes

Annex I

The District Delivery Program (DDP) 2009-2010: A Case Study in Organizational Challenges

DDP was designed to provide the "hold" and "build" phases of a COIN effort by establishing local governance and development programs after combat operations had completed the "clear" phase. In the first months of , the GOA, ISAF, and international civilians worked together to organize and implement DDP. This required considerable coordination between the many actors involved, including determining which districts to target and in what sequence, reorienting funding streams, carrying out district inventories, and working out lines of authority. Overall, DDP was a necessary part of a larger COIN effort, and was successful in some areas where it was deployed. It could be a model in other countries with active insurgencies and weak local governance.

Introduction to DDP

As the GOA, the United States, and NATO modified their strategy in 2009 towards a well-resourced, population-centric COIN strategy and increased the operational tempo in Kandahar and Helmand Provinces, the need to establish governance and carry out development programs at the district level immediately after combat operations took the form of the District Delivery Program. As part of an integrated clear-hold-build-transfer strategy, this was intended to both build infrastructure and transfer authority to Afghan district-level authorities. While this was nothing new as a concept—the IDLG, PRTs maneuver battalions and local governments had been working on similar programs for years— DDP was significant in that it aimed to address these issues on a broader, national scope, with more funds and more coordination between the Afghan interagency, international donors, and military commands. This annex will look at how DDP was initially organized in the first months of 2010, consider steps towards implementation, and offer some lessons learned and conclusions.

Definitions and Goals of DDP

The definition and goals of DDP varied somewhat depending on which government was doing the defining. As outlined by IDLG Director Popal at the 2010 London conference, "The objective of DDP is to establish or improve the visibility of the Government by holistically engaging the governance system at the district level to ensure that the basic level public services are available directly to communities."[85]

The State Department offered a slightly different definition: "This new program partners Afghan officials from critical service delivery ministries (e.g., the Ministries of Finance, Public Health, Education, Agriculture, and Rural Rehabilitation and Development) with U.S. civilian experts and ISAF to deliver an integrated package of basic services in areas recently cleared by ISAF.[86]

IDLG documents put it even more succinctly, saying that DDP intended "to demonstrate to the Afghan people that their government offers a better future than the insurgent." In addition, "the District Delivery Program is centered on two principles: 1) the Provincial Governor and District governor's offices, in conjunction with line Ministries, deliver services; and 2) that the services provided are a result of a consultative process with a local Council (representative body of the people)."[87]

USAID noted that "the DDP project represents an umbrella approach to ensuring that the reach of the Afghan central government extends to the districts. In partnership with the Independent Directorate of Local Governance and the Ministry of Finance, DDP provides support for budget planning and execution at the district level, resulting in improved delivery of key services.[88]

While some ambiguity remained (in part reflecting different thinking among the various players), DDP's purpose clearly was to establish, or reinforce, government at the district level; to provide services to the Afghans at the district level; and to provide a government presence immediately after combat operations had pushed insurgents out.

DDP's Place within the Larger Strategy

DDP was nested within a multi-layered strategic framework with both civilian and military components.[89] In a larger sense, it was also a component of the Afghan Compact. In USG channels, it was also guided by State's January 2010 "Afghanistan and Pakistan Regional Stabilization Strategy "and ultimately by President Obama's Strategy for Afghanistan and Pakistan.

Coordination and Organizational Issues

A) WHO WAS INVOLVED IN DDP?

The various organizations and embassies involved in DDP can be conceptualized as a number of intersecting "circles" (see diagram). At the center was IDLG, which was formally put in charge of DDP by a decree from President Karzai in March 2010. Intersecting with IDLG at the Kabul level were several ministries.[90] The Civil Service Commission, the Attorney General's Office, and the Supreme Court also played a role, respectively, in training civil servants and rule of law. Within the GOA, the next set of "circles" included the governors of provinces and districts where DDP was to be implemented, and the provincial representatives of ministries. Internally, IDLG created a Central Support Team to do coordination, planning and implementation, as well as "mobile advisory teams" to work in targeted provinces and districts.

Within the international community, the ISAF Joint Command (IJC) was charged with running day-to-day ISAF operations. The IJC and the US, Canadian, and British embassies— all of which provided funding to DDP—also intersected with the IDLG "circle."[91] The UNAMA also had an interest in DDP, but in the end, provided advice more than influence due to lack of funding and its policy position that DDP should extend to significantly more districts, which was opposed by several principal actors and donors.

Within the U.S Government there were several offices involved in DDP. The embassy lead was the Interagency Provincial Affairs (IPA) office, particularly its governance section, and officers from

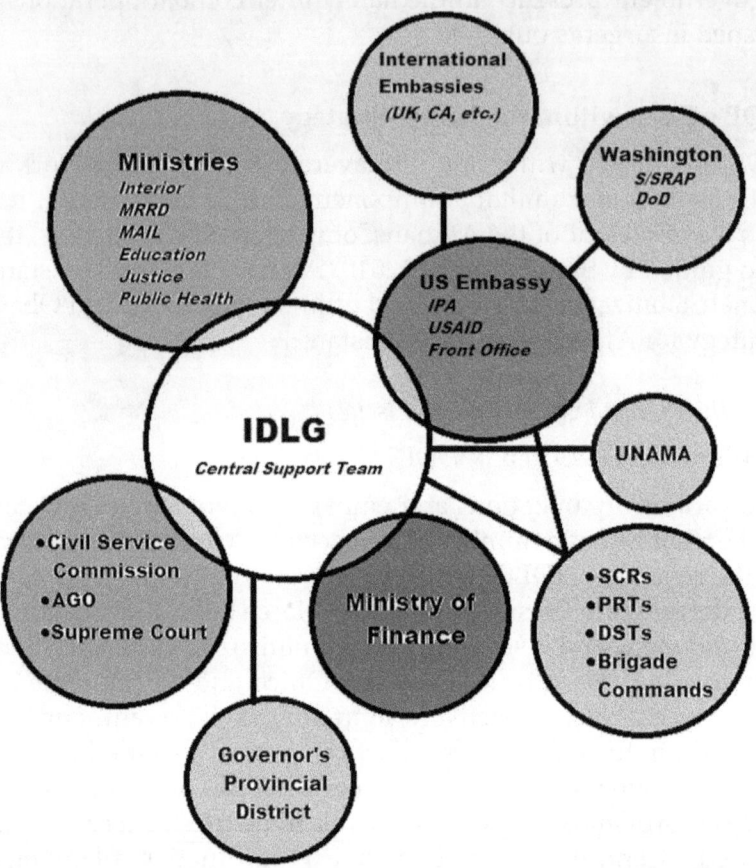

Conceptual Diagram of the Organizations Involved in DDP

USAID. Senior Civilian Representatives (SCRs) led at the level of regional commands, with civilians at brigade commands, PRTs and DSTs beneath them. On the military side, IJC's "future operations" and "information dominance cell" were heavily involved at the Kabul level.

B) ORGANIZATION STRUCTURES

The number of actors involved in DDP, both Afghan and international, and the complexity of the program itself resulted in a mix of formal and informal working groups and meetings. The IDLG hosted a weekly "DDP Planners Working Group" that included a broad variety of state actors.[92] This served as a key point for coordination, although attendance from some ministries was spotty.

To engage the field in DDP, Kabul held video conferences and conference calls for the purpose of explaining the program and what was required at various levels. The DDP program was briefed to civilian and military officers at the regional commands at Kandahar Air Field and at Bagram during day-long conferences; these were critical nodes since PRTs DSTs and maneuver units fell under these commands. Interestingly, PowerPoint slides became a tool to formulate policy and determine operations for DDP, as it forced different groups to agree on a common slide presentation. For example, IJC initially had a presentation that explained its DDP priorities and programs; this was eventually merged with the civilian views from the embassies involved. Next, the IDLG modified parts of this slide presentation with input from other ministries, which then became the official slide show for explaining and socializing DDP. The slides help achieve consensus, allowed the GOA to gain more ownership of the program, and provided more of a single "voice" for the program once this became the agreed-on presentation, particularly when given as a joint IJC/IDLG/embassy presentation.

C) IMPLEMENTATION

Prioritization

An initial challenge to DDP was determining which districts to target, in what order, and within what timeframe. This became a complex process due to the very different ideas among the many stakeholders over the relative priorities of districts, and the intended effects. The sequencing of combat operations in specific districts, or "thickening" (additional troop deployments) that DDP was, in part, intended to support was clearly a priority. IDLG, other Afghan ministries, and governors also provided input on when and where to start the program, as did the regional Senior Civilian Representatives.

IJC had already compiled a list of eighty "Key Terrain Districts" (KTDs) determined by their strategic relevancy for counter insurgency, based on population, transportation routes, and economic weight. IJC's "Operational Roadmap" set priorities and timing for these districts, and had to be modified as DDP went forward. Some of the KTDs were urban areas that were not the best fit for DDP. The city of Herat, for example, did not have ongoing combat operations and had a functioning government. At the same time, USAID was beginning to implement its Regional Afghan Municipalities Program for Urban Populations (RAMP-UP). This $600 million program provided block grants to improve services in forty-two municipalities, and further modified where DDP was to be deployed. Scheduling was also modified by some practical considerations, including security levels, feasibility in terms of personnel deployments, and USAID's ongoing realignment of programming to the various districts.

District Assessments

To effectively implement DDP, current information about the districts was needed. This included what government presence (if any) was in place, particularly district governors and representatives of line ministries, and supporting infrastructure. Local councils such as District Community Councils and District Development Assemblies, as well as any informal shuras, were surveyed. Baseline data and information on existing programs in the agriculture, justice, education, water, and health sectors was collected. The security situation and the strength of ANSF was considered, as was any international presence, particularly DSTs.

A standardized "District Inventory Matrix" was adopted for the data collection and dissemination. IDLG put together teams to do district assessments in the field, while PRTs, DSTs ,and military units were tasked with providing updated information to Kabul. Considerable background information as well as some current information already existed, requiring only that it be located, packaged, and circulated, although this proved difficult for reasons explained later in this annex. USAID also ran a District Stability Framework (DSF) program that, among other things, did assessments of districts. While not directly a part of DDP, this program was clearly related.[93]

Funding Considerations for DDP

DDP included a variety of development projects, and required that funds be realigned from existing programs, or that new funds be allocated to the districts. A general framework of three "funding streams" was devised, with on-budget, off-budget, and CERP funding streams.[94]

This realignment of GOA funds, CERP funds—controlled by U.S. Forces Afghanistan (USFOR-A)—and development funds (primarily USAID) was a considerable undertaking, but was largely completed in parallel with the prioritization of the districts. Much of the development funding was allocated to achieve a "Standardized Basic Package of Services" that included health, education, agriculture, and justice programs for each district. This Basic Package was tied to GOA guidelines relating services to population densities. For example, the guidelines called for one health center per 7,000 people, and one primary school per 1,200 students in higher-density populations.

The Ministry of Finance had the lead in funding several parts of DDP, including the operating costs of district governments, salary support for district-level officials, and "on-budget" funding to ministries for programs they would then implement at the district level. One point of discussion was the funding of salary supplements to encourage Afghan civil servants to work in the more dangerous and difficult areas, in part, because it was not seen as sustainable in the long run given the potential costs to the GOA. A related issue was the ongoing program for pay and grade reforms for civil servants, intended to standardize and, in some cases, increase salaries.

Input on budgeting of DDP projects at the provincial level was not standardized during this stage. In theory, provincial councils had an advisory role in how line ministries would spend money, as did provincial governors. In practice, the line ministries controlled their individual programs and were not required to consult with provincial-level officials.

At the Kabul level the planning and implementation of DDP required that ministries dedicate staff to the program. This caused some friction in ministries where DDP was only one of many competing priorities. IDLG in particular had to add staff, and went to the international community for funding assistance for a DDP secretariat.

D) How Did DDP Mesh with Related Programs?

As DDP was being formulated, it was clear that it must take into consideration the many programs already underway at the district and local levels. By 2010 PDPs and many DDPs had been drafted.[95] The National Solidarity Program, administered by MRRD, had been involved in more than 22,000 development projects at the grassroots level (check and expand). IDLG's Afghan Social Outreach Program (ASOP), since discontinued, sought to improve coordination between both formal and informal local governance and security forces.[96]

UNDP's National Area-Based Development Program (NABDP) also focused on governance and development at the district level.[97] The PRTs and the DSTs worked in the districts, including with CERP and AID funds. USAID had large national programs that extended to the local level, including the $360 million Afghanistan Vouchers for Increased Productive Agriculture (AVIPA) and the Local Governance and Community Development program, which was a long-term stability project for engagement with unstable areas, the fostering of hands-on local democracy, and the pre-emptive prevention of support for insurgency although this program was winding down by 2011.[98]

Some districts in the southwest where security was bad had few programs in early 2010. However, more secure areas, particularly in the east, often had multiple programs running in parallel. Fitting DDP into the existing mix of programs was a challenge, in part, because databases and lines of command often did not overlap. The district surveys outlined above helped to sort this problem out, as did AID's realignment of funding streams (since many of the programs were AID-run), along with Kabul-level consultations between donors and DDP-specific meetings.

Challenges to DDP

One of the biggest challenges to DDP was the scarcity of competent Afghan civil servants willing to live a spartan lifestyle in dangerous areas, often without their families. Pressure to move forward quickly in several difficult districts, along short timeframes, made this problem more acute. This shortage was a long-standing problem in Afghanistan due to systemic and historical factors (see chapter 5's discussion on local governance) and was the biggest bottleneck to DDP implementation. Similarly, the very limited pool of justice officials—lawyers, judges and prosecutors— stretched this system beyond what it could provide, and DDP districts were not always the highest priorities for those assigning these officers.

The ambitious schedule that resulted, in part, from the intersection of different programs (most notably DDP, KTDs and combat operations) also overstretched the Afghan system despite commendable efforts by some officials. This was apparent both at the local level and in Kabul, where some ministries missed deadlines and meetings. The IDLG upper leadership was juggling many programs, issues, and responsibilities, with DDP only one of many. In a more general sense, the GOA interagency process was still a work in progress that did not always lend itself to efficient policy formulation, although personal connections at times overcame bureaucratic inertia. For example, previously existing tensions between MRRD and IDLG were partly overcome through personal ties between the deputies of these two organizations.

DDP also had two distinct levels. Some of the DDP districts in eastern Afghanistan had been relatively stable for several years, with some government and infrastructure already in place. In contrast, some districts in Helmand and Kandahar were hotly contested, and had only minimal (or no) district government. The more developed regions may have diverted resources away from districts in the south where they were needed to implement the "hold" and "build" stages after maneuver units had completed "clearing" operations.

Allocating the correct amount of funding to districts presented several challenges. The Ministry of Finance controlled funds that had to be realigned, and had capacity bottlenecks and competing priorities that made this harder. Some GOA funds were channeled through provincial governors and on to district governors. At times, local politics entered the picture with some provincial governors favoring certain district governors, while others didn't have the necessary information or clout to get funds. As a result, some unused funds were returned from the provinces to the central government in Kabul, and the allocation cycle restarted, slowing down what was intended to be a quick and responsive program.

The collection of information and metrics on districts was difficult to carry out, and at times redundant. A large body of information already existed within various military commands; PRTs and later DSTs had been collecting information for years, and the GOA had information collected in some cases over decades. However, existing information on the districts was scattered over many databases, was sometimes classified (and hence difficult to share with the GOA and others), had not been transferred when units or officers rotated out of Afghanistan, or was in different languages. Information was also hard to share due to incompatible e-mail systems, and firewalls. Some field officers complained of parallel requests for the same information.[99] Particularly in RC-South, security issues made data collection difficult in some districts.

Informal political structures were also a factor in DDP implementation. In some districts tribes, religious leaders, influential businessmen or landowners, (as well as Taliban shadow governments) stood to lose influence if DDP implementation resulted in improved governance and provision of services. Similarly, many Afghans viewed the GOA with suspicion, in part, due to corruption problems,[100] and did not always view an increased government presence as a good thing. This situation may have been made more difficult by the postponement (for various reasons) of district-level elections, which resulted in District Governors being appointed. These were complex problems that, in the end, will need to be resolved by Afghans.

Within Afghan ministries at the Kabul level, turf wars and pre-existing suspicions had an impact on DDP. In the end personal relations (particularly at the deputies level), the involvement of the international community, and a series of planning meetings helped to lessen any negative impacts. Although IDLG had the lead for planning and implementing DDP, it in fact had very little authority over other ministries, who could ignore its guidance.[101]

Expectation management was an issue—the multiple bottlenecks that slowed DDP came as a surprise to some in the international community, causing frustration and leading to adjustment of plans. The idea that a "government in a box" was available for immediate deployment, as believed by some, had to be changed.

After DDP was deployed to the challenging Helmand district

of Marja, IDLG carried out a "lessons learned" exercise.[102] To paraphrase the main points:

- Given the number of players at the national, provincial and district levels, a strong monitoring system was necessary to determine what was going right, and to provide information on what was going wrong.
- Security at the local level was key to DDP, and the MOI was the key player in providing security for the civil servants.
- Provincial and District Governors offices needed adequate capacity to do planning, project assessment, and reporting.
- The upper limits of funding need to be established, to avoid wish-lists of projects that, in the end, would not be funded.
- Better public relations campaigns were needed to adequately inform the population about DDP, and of progress being made.
- DDP should be a catalyst for existing national programs, rather than a standalone program.
- Consulting the local population and gaining buy-in from the start for programs and projects was critical.

In a more general sense, the pre-existing tensions and differing priorities within the international community—military, civilian, and various governments—were a significant challenge to DDP. While these tensions were not resolved, they could be managed, which was the case with the DDP start-up. One example was UNAMA officers pushing to have DDP extended nationwide, including to many peaceful districts. Because of the specific focus of DDP on key districts, and the limits of funding and resources, this was not practicable, but in the end UNAMA understood this and remained part of the process. Some IDLG officials saw differences between IJC and the U.S. embassy over lists of districts as an impediment.[103] At the same time, ISAF and Gen. McChrystal were under pressure to show momentum and results after the 2009 shift to a population-centric COIN approach was put in place; in turn, DDP was under pressure to move quickly and gave this program the necessary attention and resources.

The private Afghanistan Research and Evaluation Unit analyzed the start of DDP in 2010 with this astute summary: "The roll out of this program has required intensive organization and cooperation between all parties. Two primary difficulties have been the recruitment and retention of suitably qualified civil servants to work in the districts, and establishing mechanisms that allow funds to be delivered through government fiscal systems and operational budgets with sufficient speed to allow the program to move forward and staff to be paid. Both issues are being addressed; district line ministries are operating with increased coordination and impetus in response to staffing challenges, while efforts to overcome blockages impeding the flow of funds from the Ministry of Finance down through line ministries to province and district level have served to increase system efficiency. A further problem caused by the DDP was the pressure that this rapid injection of resources placed on ministries already hard pressed to meet their national mandate.[104]

Conclusions Regarding the District Delivery Program

The DDP program would have been difficult to organize and implement even a few years earlier because many of the human, organizational and financial pieces were not yet in place. However, by 2010 both the GOA and the international community had adequate capacity to make DDP run. For example, IDLG was only instituted in 2007, and had only gradually gained the capacity to match its many responsibilities; only by 2009 or 2010 could it have taken on a program as large as DDP. While the USG and NATO/ISAF had engaged in counterinsurgency programs for years, in 2009 a more fully resourced, population-centric COIN strategy was adopted, which set the stage for DDP. Also, civil-military coordination between USFOR-A, ISAF and embassy staffs, important for this program, had been gradually evolving and improving. This was in part due to organizational changes (led largely by Ambassador Eikenberry) that matched U.S. civil and military officers from the highest ranks in Kabul down to DSTs, and in part through practical experience, as officers did multiple tours in Afghanistan (and Iraq) and learned to work with their counterparts. Importantly, U.S. civilian staffing had been expanded as part of a "civilian surge," improving the likelihood that DDP would receive the attention it needed both in Kabul and in the field. An Afghan interagency process to coordinate between ministries was gradually evolving, and by 2010 functioned enough to support DDP. Finally, the will to do this program was there—while the international community often had to push, many Afghans also wanted this program to work.

While short to medium-term gains could be consolidated with help from ISAF troops and international development funds, longer term gains will obviously be harder, depending on ANSF, ministries and the commitment and competence of local officials. Clearly, gains could be lost if local government doesn't function (particularly in delivering services) or is viewed as predatory, corrupt or unresponsive to the population.

A more general consideration is if DDP was the best approach in areas where the local preference is for an informal system of government, and/or there is mistrust of the Afghan government. Similarly, was focusing on the district level correct in areas where the international community would soon reduce its presence through DSTs, and shift back to more of a provincial-level presence? This may become apparent as soon as 2014, when the international presence is reduced and the GOA will lead on any further implementation of the program.

The considerable effort required to initiate DDP was a "forcing function" that made many national and international parties work together. This may have the unintended benefit of making it easier to run other complex programs in the future—although the rapid turnover of international officers could diminish this effect. Another practical effect of this program could be to formally grant more local decision making and operational capacity to local levels, since Afghanistan, at least on paper, is one of the most centralized states in the world.[105] Local needs can almost certainly be better met by tailoring programs locally, rather than through larger programs directed from Kabul. Local programs that deliver services—education, health, and agriculture extension, for example—are also something the insurgents generally cannot supply (although justice at times is an exception).

While conditions in Pakistan are considerably different than Afghanistan, programs similar to DDP could support COIN and stabilization programs in the FATA and other border areas. U.S. and international funds could be designated to support such a program, through existing provincial and local government bodies.

As the international community reduces its security presence, one option is to expand local security forces at the district level. These programs, such as the Afghan Local Police program have parallels with DDP—both are local programs with ties into district and provincial government, and with some oversight and support from Kabul. DDP lessons learned may be relevant, particularly solutions to moving funds at the ministerial level and then to the provinces. As with DDP, ASP/local defense programs may be difficult to run without increased capacity in various ministries, particularly the MOI, and at the provincial government level. Similarly, ISAF forces performed a coordinating function for DDP; in the future, coordination between civilian ministries and the ANA and ANP will be needed to make local defense programs run.

Overall, DDP was a necessary program to support the COIN strategy by building up local governance structures (or bolstering existing local governance), while consolidating gains made through combat operations. Previously, many combat operations had to be repeated after "cleared" areas reverted to insurgent control when Afghan political, development and security forces did not solidify, or were forced to leave by insurgents. DDP was a needed component of the take-hold-build-transfer concept, one that hopefully the GOA will be able to sustain over the long term with help from the international community. According to a former high-ranking Afghan government official, by early 2012 DDP was already functioning well in Kandahar, Helmand and Nangarhar.[106] It may also serve as a model for other countries that are coping with complex situations involving insurgencies, weak governance, and ongoing combat operations, coupled with large-scale international programs.

Annex II

Khost Province in 2004-2005: A Case Study in Operations along the Border with Pakistan

In Khost province during the period 2004–2005, conventional maneuver battalions, a PRT, a Brigade Command and Special Operations Forces carried out a largely successful counterinsurgency campaign. This contributed to the expansion of the local economy, the Afghan government increasing its reach and capacity, and the holding of two successful elections. The Haqqani network, the predominant insurgent group in the area, was unable to make significant inroads, although by 2005 this was changing rapidly. Post-2007 the US expanded its focus on the province, leading to considerable progress, and Khost being held up as a model of COIN by late 2007. However, the Haqqanis were also gaining operational capability, eventually resulting in considerable violence in the province, making the expansion of government and development programs much more difficult.

Khost Province: Culture, Economic and Security Situation

Khost is a relatively small province roughly 120 air miles south of Kabul, with a population of about 600,000, according to MRRD statistics. To the east and north lie the North Waziristan and Kurram agencies of the FATA of Pakistan. Khost's population is almost entirely Pashtun. A strong tribal structure remains, with a complex and shifting network of rivalries and alliances.

Khost's society was evolving rapidly as its traditional, insular culture was exposed to new ideas and technologies. Expatriate workers and former refugees were returning, bringing with them a broader view of the world. However, Pashtun culture remained strong, including the obligation for revenge and hospitality, as well as the high value of family and tribal honor. Tribal law was still widely followed, intermingled with conventional law. Women's rights remained very restricted, and traditional mores were harshly enforced.

The center of the province is an elongated valley, surrounded by rugged hills and mountains. Rivers and streams provide sufficient water to keep the valley bottom irrigated, and farmers grow wheat, rice, sorghum, fruits and nuts, and raise livestock. During the period 2004–2005, poppy production was minimal. Khost has always lacked sufficient infrastructure, and twenty-five years of war had degraded what existed—roads were poor, and the health and education system was weak or nonexistent in some places. The electric system was based on private generators, and there was no electric grid. In 2004, the economy was largely tied to Pakistan, although by 2005, with the improvement of roads and the growth of the Afghan economy, this was changing.

During the period 2004–2005, U.S. Army and Marine units provided the vast majority of Coalition forces in Khost, with support provided by aviation units, including attack aviation, medical evacuation, and logistical flights. Afghan security forces included the Afghan National Army (ANA), Afghan National Police (ANP) and Afghan Militia Force units, as well as tribal militias.

In Pakistan, the under-funded and poorly trained Frontier Corps was deployed along the border. The Pakistani Army was increasingly active in Waziristan, carrying out sweeps against some insurgent groups, particularly those with foreign fighters, and providing security in support of Afghan elections.

Operating out of adjacent North Waziristan, the Haqqanis intensified their operations in Khost beginning in the spring of 2005. In particular, IED attacks were more frequent and more sophisticated, possibly reflecting technology and tactics brought from Iraq. The insurgents also increased coordinated attacks on patrols, indirect fire on bases, propaganda campaigns, and attacks on pro-government and pro-coalition Afghans. They also carried out operations to destroy Coalition-funded projects, and began to expand their reach into neighboring Paktika Province as well.

al-Qaeda previously used Khost as a training and staging area, and may have been involved in some operations. Other cross border attacks may have been carried out by foreign jihadists, including Uzbeks, Arabs, and Punjabis, or were "graduation exercises" for radical madrassas. Despite this complex and serious security situation, U.S. forces were able to operate effectively.

Military and Civilian Components in Khost Province

Khost Provincial Reconstruction Team (PRT)

The Khost PRT was established in early 2004. Of the eight RC-East PRTs, it was one of the smallest, with between eighty and 100 soldiers and civilians, plus a number of Afghan employees. Most PRTs were commanded by a lieutenant colonel, but during most of the period 2004–2005 Khost was commanded by a very able reserve major, an investment banker in civilian life. The Khost PRT mission statement, similar to that of other PRTs, read: "conduct Civil Military Operations to improve security, facilitate reconstruction, and promote economic development in order to extend the reach and legitimacy of the central government and to create an environment conducive for a successful parliamentary election." While a seemingly simple statement, in fact this resulted in a wide spectrum of activities – the PRT became a versatile tool, reacting to the situation on the ground as needed.

As with other OEF PRTs Khost had two main civil-military components: a Civilian Affairs Team-Alpha (CAT-A) and a Civil-Military Operations Center (CMOC). The CAT-A, headed by a captain, focused at the district level, maintaining contacts with district sub-governors, tribal leaders, police chiefs and mullahs. These engagements identified immediate impact projects as well as potential reconstruction and development projects. Most projects were small—less than the $25,000 CERP limit. The CAT-A team's activities had the added benefit of providing presence patrols, which strengthened the confidence of local people, supported the district government, and restricted the ability of insurgents to set up shadow governments.

The CMOC, located in a compound in the center of Khost city and headed by a senior NCO, had multiple responsibilities. It provided a point of contact for locals who wanted to approach the PRT (although many went directly to the PRT headquarters instead), acted as a contracting office for PRT projects, and provided a venue for meetings with government officials. The CMOC had a colonel from the MOI permanently assigned to it, providing liaison with the local police forces.

Khost Maneuver Battalions

During the period 2004–2005, three maneuver battalions operated in Khost—the 3rd Battalion, 3rd Marines, the 2nd Battalion, 3rd Marines, and the 2nd Battalion, 504th Infantry of the 82nd Airborne Division. These units also had Paktia and Logar Provinces in their areas of operation. In contrast to the lightly armed PRTs, which only engaged in combat operations when forced to by enemy action, the maneuver units were fully geared for combat operations. These maneuver units also supported the Afghan government during emergency operations, including riots, armed tribal disputes, floods, and the periodic influx of large numbers of Afghan refugees after camps in Pakistan were closed.

In Khost, considerable effort was put on counter-insurgency in a few border districts, as much of the province away from the border was fairly stable, including the city of Khost. Security operations usually took the form of patrols, cordon and search operations, and the establishment of temporary "patrol bases" to provide an extended presence. In areas with active insurgencies, larger operations were carried out, sometimes using helicopter-borne troops to block insurgent movements. Units also engaged in counter-IED operations, and seizures of weapons caches. These efforts also helped to secure "humanitarian space by" providing enough security that the PRT, and to some extent, the Afghan government, were able to operate effectively.

Aside from air support and heavy artillery, the maneuver units were largely self-supporting, with a command center separate from the brigade command, and a full staff. Requests for air support were channeled through the brigade command. The maneuver battalions were led by a lieutenant colonel, whose duties often extended into political and civil-military affairs, dealing with governors, ministry officials, and tribal leaders.

While their primary focus was counter-insurgency, the battalions also had modified "CAT-A" civil-affairs units, and a CERP budget for small projects. These projects often targeted populations in areas with active insurgencies, with the aim of demonstrating the benefits of supporting the GOA and the Coalition Battalion officers also contributed to political development; the commanders were often in close contact with governors and police chiefs, in some cases acting as de facto advisors. In addition, company commanders—usually captains—worked at the district level, developing relations with sub-governors, mullahs and tribal leaders.

Special Forces Units

The Special Forces had an ODB at Khost, and ODA deployed, which included elements at several FOBs. These units engaged in targeted attacks on insurgent leaders and forces, training of Afghan security forces, psychological operations, and reconstruction efforts. At times, these forces cooperated closely with the battalions and PRT efforts, which complemented the limited manpower of the ODAs while bringing a high level of expertise to shared operations.

Afghan Security Forces

The Afghan government deployed three main security forces in Khost: the ANA, ANP, and the NDS. Subordinate to the ANP were the Highway Police and the Border Police, although these units were not present in many areas. Of these forces, the ANA was overall the most effective, and the most respected by the populace. However, the ANA was not deployed in significant numbers in Khost until the spring of 2005. The ANP was often lacking in equipment, funding and morale; they were also perceived by much of the population as being corrupt in various degrees. In general, relations between the Afghan forces and the PRTs and maneuver units were cooperative.

Informal Afghan Forces

In addition to the formal security forces, there were a variety of informal units present. In the Pashtun areas there still existed the tradition of tribal *alberkai* militias raised to provide security for specific events or emergencies. These were mustered for both the presidential and parliamentary elections, and performed well at the village level. Several tribal and local strongmen still controlled their own informal militias, but by the end of 2005, these had mostly been disbanded. In some areas, existing militias were endorsed by the government and Coalition until the ANA could take over; an example where this worked well was the 25th Afghan Militia Force, a battalion-sized unit, based in Khost.

Civilian Components

U. S. Department of State Political Officers

The State Department assigned political officers to both the PRTs and the Brigade headquarters in Khost, assigning them four main tasks. First, and most importantly, they did what they could to extend the reach of the central government in Kabul and improve the effectiveness of the local government. Second, they were reporting officers, tasked with providing information on political, political-military, economic, and social trends to the embassy in Kabul. Third, they were conduits of information for the military, on various topics—what U.S. government, State Department and the embassy policies were, what was happening in Afghanistan at the national level, and information on developments in Pakistan, a very relevant topic for the border provinces. Fourth, they were charged with promoting U.S. government policies to the provincial government. The political officer traveled with the commanders, meeting with political leaders (usually the governor) as well as military leaders.

USAID and USDA

USAID officers, designated as Field Program Officers, were assigned to both the PRT and Brigade command in Khost. These officers were responsible for administering USAID projects at the provincial level, advising military officers on development issues, advising the federal government on long-term reconstruction and development strategy, and reporting back to AID headquarters in Kabul. USDA officers focused on providing agricultural advice to the Afghan government, and to a lesser extent to individual farmers.

International Civilian Component — UNAMA

UNAMA had hub offices at Gardez that covered several provinces, including Khost. UNAMA officers had a wide mandate, dealing with conflict prevention and resolution, monitoring of human rights, promotion of elections and building government capacity. The lead political officers worked closely with U.S. political and military officers.

The "Three Pillars" in Khost: Security, Economic and Strategic Reconstruction, Governance and Justice

U.S. efforts in Khost followed "three-pillar" counter insurgency strategy established by CFC-A. With guidance from the brigade command, the Khost PRT focused on security, economic and strategic reconstruction, and governance and justice. While this was a complex effort involving many actors, the following section focuses on the PRT's role.

1) Security

Improving security was one of three main "pillars" of the Khost PRT's mission statement, but in the end maneuver battalions and other actors, provincially and regionally—eventually including the ANA—were the driving forces in this area. The PRT's efforts could be divided into three main areas: police training and assistance; support for disarmament and reconciliation programs; and a weakly defined but important role as an "honest broker" in provincial security affairs. Police Technical Advisory Teams (PTATs) provided the primary security training effort of the PRT. These teams were manned by reservists who were police officers at home, or by regular Military Police officers. They provided practical training to ANP and ABP officers on basic police functions—patrolling, searching people and cars, crowd and riot control, collection of evidence, administration, and weapons. The Special Forces ODAs and conventional maneuver units reinforced the PTAT training during their patrols in the districts. The PTATs taught much-needed classes on ethics, in hopes of countering rampant corruption of the police and reducing the abuse of citizens by the police. They were also the mechanism for using CERP funding to provide radios, facilities, fuel, and vehicles.

The PRT also helped facilitate several federal and internationally backed security programs. The largest of these was the national Disarmament, Demobilization, and Reintegration (DDR) program. In Khost, the focus of this effort was the 25th Afghan Militia Force, a well-armed unit of perhaps 500 local men, led by the wily, Soviet-trained General Kiel Baz. The PRT helped redeploy some of these fighters into other military units, and facilitated the reentry of others into civilian life. The Afghan government's reconciliation program was active in Khost; the PRT worked closely with the governor to encourage Taliban fighters to peacefully reenter society, and with the tribes to assure their good behavior once back in civilian life—a strong incentive. By mid-2005, the national DIAG program was underway, with the PRT involved in disarming the few warlords who remained in the Khost area. All of these initiatives were done in coordination with the maneuver battalion, Special Forces, and to some extent, the brigade command.

The least defined, but most important and successful security role of the PRT, was as a mediator within Afghan society. Khost suffered from numerous tribal and land disputes (aggravated by multiple, conflicting land titles produced under different regimes over the previous 25 years). PRT officers, working with Afghan and Coalition forces, were able to assist in defusing disputes between the heavily armed tribes, and in some cases helped delineate tribal boundaries. In addition, Afghan security forces lacked coordination, at times due to personal differences between commanders; the PRT was able to act as a "bridge", and improve coordination between the ANP, ABP, and eventually the ANA. The PRT also shamed blatantly corrupt police officers, and pushed for the removal of the worst. Finally, by being a neutral player that could, as necessary, call on substantial Coalition military, economic, and political resources if provincial affairs got badly out of control, the PRT provided an intangible but very real confidence booster to the national COIN apparatus.

Analysis of Security Efforts

By late 2005, the security situation in Khost had become more difficult as the insurgents improved their coordination, and deployed more numerous and more sophisticated IEDs. However, at the same time, Afghan security forces were steadily improving, the lid was kept on tribal conflicts, and the insurgents were limited in what they could do. The efforts of PRT and maneuver battalion officers, closely coordinated, were a significant factor in these successes.

2) Economic and Strategic Reconstruction

Due to security concerns, NGOs and multilateral organizations such as the World Bank had almost no presence in Khost during the period 2004–2005. At the same time, USAID encountered significant problems in delivering on its planned projects, in part, due to difficulties with its chief implementing partner, the IOM. As a result, the CERP projects administered by the PRT and maneuver battalions took on considerable significance. Improving the mostly dirt road from Khost north to Gardez was a focus for AID, but this was a long-term, expensive program that did not make much progress during this time.

Government of Afghanistan

While the ministry representatives tasked with reconstruction and development had good intentions, the Afghan government was severely strapped for funds, and lacked the capacity to carry out large-scale projects or sustain projects funded by the coalition. PRT officers (including the AID officer) worked with these ministries to increase their capabilities. One important outcome was a five-year development plan for the province, which prioritized needs and assigned responsibility between the Coalition (including AID) and the various ministries.

CERP

The PRT and maneuver battalions both carried out an extensive program of small projects funded by CERP, with the PRT as the predominant player. Projects included schools, health clinics, water wells, the refurbishment of mosques and shrines, the improvement of market areas, improvement of roads (particularly a hub-and-spoke system to connect the districts to Khost town), and irrigation systems. The military's Overseas Humanitarian, Disaster, and Civic Aid (OHDACA) funding was used for a few larger school and hospital projects.

Others

Health care in the city of Khost was rudimentary at best and almost nonexistent in some rural areas. AID, in its most effective program in Khost, provided substantial support to the hospital in town, and also began a badly needed midwives training program. In addition, the PRT, maneuver units, and Special Forces coordinated an effective series of medical civic action programs (MEDCAPs) in the districts, where military doctors and medics would treat hundreds of patients.

Analysis of Economic and Strategic Reconstruction Efforts

CERP projects were a success story in Khost, filling a gap that traditional development players were unable to address, helping the Afghans, and providing a valuable counterinsurgency tool. However, the province needed long-term development assistance, to include large road, dam and electricity projects beyond the scope of CERP.

3) Governance and Justice

One clear success story on both the political and public relations fronts were the monthly meetings held with mullahs from throughout the province, attended by PRT, battalion, and Special Forces officers. These gave each side a chance to present their views on a variety of issues—forced entry to houses by security forces, the IED threat, elections, or corruption in government, for example. The meetings were held on Thursdays, so that the mullahs could include what was discussed in their Friday sermons.

This concept was expanded to include separate meetings with ministry representatives, district sub-governors, tribal leaders, and businessmen. As with the mullah's meetings, these provided an opportunity to transmit and receive information, mediate disputes, prod government officials to act or shame them to not steal public funds, or to support Kabul's programs. The meetings were also useful for "damage control" if a Coalition operation went wrong and resulted in civilian casualties.

The brigade command, in conjunction with the PRTs, State, and AID officers, hosted a series of governors' conferences, pulling together the governors of Khost, Ghazni, Paktia, and Paktika. These meetings were intended to build security and economic ties between provinces, discuss development priorities, increase the effectiveness of reconciliation efforts, and build ties between officials at the federal level.

Public relations were a factor in the success or failure of PRT and maneuver battalion operations and an area of struggle with the insurgents. In Khost, where much of the population remains illiterate, rumors spread quickly, and disinformation campaigns could quickly cause real damage to Coalition efforts. Radio was the chief means to counter Taliban efforts, given the lack of television and the limited availability of print media.

Presidential and Parliamentary Elections

The presidential elections, held in October 2004, and the parliamentary and provincial council elections, held in September 2005, were complex operations, carried out over several months in challenging terrain, among a population still unfamiliar with democratic fundamentals, and in the face of threats from the insurgents to disrupt them. In the end, these elections took place largely as planned, and were very successful, returning credible results. The Afghan people, through their enthusiasm for the elections, made them a success, but the detailed planning and execution of government and Coalition elements, coupled with those of the UN and contractors, enabled this success.

In Khost, coordination between the various players began months before the elections, usually through meetings held at the PRT, Governor's compound, Joint Electoral Management Body (JEMB) offices, Brigade Headquarters, or in the field at polling stations or counting centers. The Coalition made support of the elections one of its highest priorities. This support took many forms. The brigade command dedicated considerable manpower to planning security and support for voter registration, transport of ballots, security of voting and registration sites, interdiction of Taliban efforts, and security of counting centers (not only in Khost, but throughout its AO). The maneuver units increased their operational tempo, keeping the insurgents off balance, and easing the workload for the Afghan forces.

Some of the maneuver units' most successful operations were "governor's tours," where U.S. and Afghan forces escorted Governor Patan throughout the province prior to the elections. These gave the governor an opportunity to explain the purpose and process of the elections (as the governor was appointed by Kabul, he was not running for office himself), while also extending the presence of the provincial government to the more remote districts.

The PRT played a major role at the provincial level, setting up a command center where all Afghan, Coalition and private contractors were represented. This center was the communications node on election day and coordinated responses to breaking events. The State Department political officer was active in election preparations, advising the military on the mechanics of the electoral process, keeping abreast of political developments, participating in planning meetings, working closely with UNAMA and JEMB, and going on the "governor's tours."

Analysis of Coalition Support for Elections

Coalition forces, with their considerable resources, made a major contribution to the success of both elections. Particularly in the more remote districts and those with active insurgencies, their very presence reduced or precluded attacks on election workers, voters, candidates, and counting centers. This was done while keeping the maximum Afghan "face" on security efforts—federal forces, bolstered by tribal *alberkai* militias, had the lead at all levels. In the end, security incidents were minimal across the region. An unanticipated but notable success was that the elections forced the Afghan forces—ANA, ANP and NDS—to coordinate their operations. The

Coalition helped make this happen, through organizing joint patrols, holding countless planning meetings in the run up to the elections, and hosting the provincial command centers.

Interagency Cooperation

During the years 2004 and 2005, coordination between the PRT, maneuver battalions, Special Forces, brigade command, and U.S. government civilians was quite good, and was a factor in successes in Khost province. This coordination extended into all three of the counter-insurgency "pillars"—security, development, and political. Personal relations between commanders were important, given the need to adjust to rapidly changing situations on the ground, and the still ad-hoc organizational structures. For example, the PRT commander and the Special Forces commander worked very closely together, with a standing meeting scheduled every evening. The presence of the brigade commander in Khost also smoothed relations by providing an authoritative arbiter of any disputes over operations and responsibilities.

Conclusions

The combined efforts of OEF units, U.S. government officers, GOA, and international organizations made a significant difference in Khost in 2004 and 2005. Overall, the economy expanded, the federal government increased its reach and capacity, two successful elections were held, and the insurgents were unable to make significant inroads. Numerous problems remained, including endemic corruption, rivalries between tribes, instability in Pakistan and attendant cross-border attacks, a more effective insurgency, low government revenues, and an overall low level of infrastructure. Decades of work remained, but a leap of progress was made during this time period.

While any metrics of success in such a complex situation will be difficult to assess, there may be a few telltale signs for both Khost and all of eastern Afghanistan. If maneuver battalions become more important, the insurgents will be winning. In contrast, if PRTs, NGOs and Afghan ministries involved in development take the lead in more provinces, this will show the insurgents are failing. Similarly, the amount of battle space the ANA can take over, and the degree to which it can secure the "humanitarian space" for NGOs, will be an indicator of how well this critical force is progressing. Afghans in border provinces realize their very survival often depends on being aligned with the stronger side. The proportion of Afghans siding with the GOA and coalition, or with the insurgents, will be a critical trend. At the same time, the average Afghans view of the government—whether it is perceived as corrupt or honest, effective or ineffective, representative or predatory—will be an indicator of success. As in most countries, Afghans will vote their pocketbooks, and if they do not perceive tangible economic benefits and a hopeful economic future, they may not only throw out the Karzai government but the democratic model. Education indicators will also be telling. It is unlikely that democracy will flourish in the long term if Afghanistan does not reach some critical mass of educated voters. A negative indicator will be the number of parents sending their children to madrassas, particularly across the border to Pakistan.

Epilogue

After 2005 Khost had years in which considerable progress was made, and then setbacks as the insurgency gained strength. By 2012, the discussion centered on the fate of Khost after the 2014 drawdown of U.S. and NATO troops, and if the province could be held by Afghan troops (personal communication with former U.S. ambassador, summer 2012).[107] A study based on interviews with US commanders and civilian officials noted the following:

> US forces made significant progress in Khost in 2006 and 2007. The "Khost model" demonstrated many good counterinsurgency practices, such as the dispersion of forces into small patrol bases in population centers, constant patrols with Afghan forces, and close coalition coordination. . . .Unfortunately, the gains made by coalition forces from 2006 to early 2008 were too fragile. Intensified insurgent attacks in conjunction with unit rotations, less coalition coordination, the loss of an effective governor, and increased

US activity across the border undid much of what had been accomplished. As security declined, the people of Khost began to doubt that the coalition still had the momentum. Stepped-up raids and clearing operations by the coalition also contributed to a decline in popular support. Ultimately, it was premature to call the operation in Khost a model of a successful counterinsurgency after only two years of progress.[108]

As a sign of how dangerous Khost was becoming, five different attempts were made to assassinate Governor Arsala Jamal, in office from August 2006 to November 2008 (These attacks eventually found their mark–Jamal was appointed Governor of Logar Province in April 2013, and was killed in a bomb attack there in October 2103).

Interestingly, in the mid-1980s the Soviets faced similar challenges in Khost, with mujahedeen crossing from Pakistan, and also operating from the base at Zhawar, in Khost province near the Pakistani border. At the same time, the Soviets had to struggle to keep the road to Gardez open, particularly through the pass half-way between the towns. As noted in the book "The Battle for Afghanistan," "the Soviet border strategy [in Khost] was based on maintaining a multitude of posts large and small, close to Pakistan. They were intended to seal the border and interdict [mujahedeen] supply routes. It was rather like a person trying to shut off a large tap by putting his hand over it. Throughout the war the majority of these garrisons have been under at least partial siege…" He adds that "…with hindsight, these towns and posts probably diverted our efforts too much from Kabul, and other more suitable guerilla targets." At the same time, a mujahedeen offensive in 1985 was unable to take the city of Khost in the face of superior firepower.[109]

Annex III

Three Case Studies in Civil-Military Cooperation as a Function of Security, 2004-2005

This section will use case studies to analyze how the level of security determined what combinations of Afghan Government, PRTs, maneuver units, international organizations, and Special Forces were used in different areas for different goals.

U.S. counterinsurgency efforts in eastern Afghanistan in 2004 and 2005 were predominantly focused on the provinces bordering Pakistan, where the majority of combat operations took place. The provinces with the most active insurgencies were Khost, Paktika, and Konar Provinces, with security generally improving away from the border and in non-Pashtun areas, such as Bamian and Panjshir Provinces.

The situation in many provinces, particularly those near the border with Pakistan, was often unstable and rapidly changing. Provincial governance was weak, with limited reach into the districts, and tribal leaders and local strongmen often filled power vacuums. Cross-border attacks were common in some areas, particularly in Khost and Paktika, and by the summer of 2005, the insurgents had increased their numbers, command and control, and armaments. Suicide bombings, previously a rare occurrence, happened more frequently beginning in the spring of 2005. The ANA, though lacking anywhere near the required number of *kandaks* (battalions), gradually increased its presence in several provinces. The ANP continued to struggle, hampered by insufficient equipment, poor pay, high levels of corruption, and in many cases, poor leadership.

Case Study 1— Bermel Valley: Maneuver Battalion Leads

The Bermel Valley, in the far eastern reaches of Paktika province, is a rocky desert, with low mountain ranges to the east and west. Across the border is Pakistan's FATA South Waziristan agency, a hotbed of insurgent activity, apparently based in the town of Wana. Several mountain valleys have streams that support limited agriculture, but otherwise the economy is based on trade, particularly cross-border commerce.

The Waziri tribe is predominant in this area and extends into Pakistan. The Durand line has split this tribe, and in some sense, Bermel district is an extension of Waziristan. Historically, the government of Afghanistan has never had strong control of this district. Twice during the period 2002–2004 the ANP had been driven off by insurgents, in one case with several officers killed. Complicating the picture, only a poor road connected Bermel with the rest of Afghanistan. The insurgents utilized stretches of this road for ambush sites. In 2004, a PRT convoy was ambushed on this road, and sustained several casualties in a firefight that lasted more than an hour.

In 2003, the U.S. 2-27 IN maneuver battalion maintained a company in the area, a period during which there was minimal combat activity; later the AO was passed to a Special Forces unit. The porous border with Pakistan, frequent cross-border insurgent attacks, and rocket barrages made the Bermel district difficult to secure. Added to the mix were intertribal rivalries between the Kharoti and Waziri tribes, and the tendency of people on the border to be "fence sitters", reluctant to trust their future to either the Coalition or the Afghan government, for fear of an insurgent return.

In early 2005, Governor Mohanmand Gulab Mangal of Paktika decided to reestablish a district government in Bermel, and requested assistance from the U.S. military. A decision was made at the brigade level to support this request, and the 1-508 IN (which had taken over Paktika from the 2-27 IN) was tasked with the operation, in coordination with Special Forces. The provincial government, the commander of the 1-508 IN, and tribal elders first hammered out a political agreement, guaranteeing the support of the tribes, providing a parcel of land for a government center, and agreeing that each tribe provide men for a security force.

By late spring, elements of a company arrived in Bermel Bazaar, roughly 15 km. north of the town of Shkin, and began setting up a perimeter in a patch of desert outside of town. Over the following weeks, a district sub-government was established (headed by a bold ex-police officer from Paktia province), and provincial ANP and ABP units arrived. This was followed by the construction of barracks, a government center, a medical post, and a mosque. This operation was important for several reasons. It directly extended the reach of the provincial government into an area where its writ had not only been contested, but effectively removed by insurgents. It also took the fight directly to the insurgents based in South Waziristan, putting Afghan and Coalition forces close to their sanctuaries, and providing a buffer for the remainder of Paktika province.

Analysis

Bermel was a case where a very tenuous security situation required that the maneuver battalion, supported by Special Forces, take the lead instead of the PRT. Although the goal of "extending the reach of the Government of Afghanistan" fell within the PRT's responsibilities, the PRT lacked the firepower and resources to take on the job. The State Department's role was limited—the officer assigned to the brigade command in Khost was involved in the initial planning, and made several trips to Bermel to assess the situation. At this time, there was no State political officer assigned to either the PRT in Sharan, or the maneuver battalion in Orgun-E. Either or both would have put an extra "tool in the toolbox," particularly during the negotiations with tribal leaders prior to the operation, and subsequently in helping establish the district government. The AID officer in Sharan contributed by working to arrange funding for the district government center. By late 2007 the Bermel firebase had grown to include a U.S. battalion headquarters, the district government center, a mosque, and an ANA base. This was a successful operation that provided security and governance to a tough district, while also interdicting the cross-border flow of insurgents.

Case Study 2—United Nations Leads on Regional Issues

UNAMA maintained two regional offices in the RC-East—in Gardez and Jalalabad. These offices kept good contacts with the governors and tribes, as well as the USG. The Gardez office worked closely with U.S. military and civilian officers to plan and execute the so-called "Zadran Arc Initiative", targeted at the districts where the Zadran tribe has influence—where Khost, Paktia, and Paktika Provinces come together. The UNAMA officer responsible for the project saw the need to reduce tension among the various tribes, while expanding the influence of the governors and engaging U.S. development funds. To that end, he worked closely with tribal leaders and the three provincial governors to broker a peace deal between the tribes (in part, by delineating boundaries of tribal lands), with the governors and tribal leaders signing a formal agreement. The U.S. military provided additional support, hosting several regional governors' conferences, and providing funding for projects in the area under CERP. The Zadran Arc Initiative helped secure the pass between Khost and Gardez, keeping an important logistical route open and improving security along the route of a planned $100 million USAID road-building project.

The United Nations High Commissioner for Refugees (UNHCR), the UN Refugee Agency, led in Khost in the spring and summer of 2005, when several Afghan Refugee camps located across the border in Pakistan were closed on short notice. UNHCR took the lead in coordinating efforts with the Afghan Government and U.S. forces, including the Khost PRT, while also providing some logistical support for the returnees. Interestingly, tribal and village ties played a major role in absorbing the returnees back into society.

Case Study 3—Afghan Government Leads on Elections, with Significant International Support

The presidential elections, held in October 2004, and the parliamentary and provincial council elections, held in September 2005, were both complex operations, requiring considerable planning and logistical efforts over periods of several months. At the same time, the very nature of the event required complete Afghan participation, and the lead of the Afghan government. In support of the elections were a wide range of participants—UNAMA, JEMB, the PRTs, maneuver battalions and Task Force commands, Afghan security forces, and international contractors, along with considerable community involvement.

Analysis

UNAMA political officers brought considerable background and skill to their work; however, their offices often lacked adequate staff to fully carry out the responsibilities assigned to them by their Kabul office, and in a larger sense, by the Bonn Agreement. In the end, the resources brought to bear by the brigade commands both overshadowed the UNAMA efforts, and also drew the UNAMA officers to try and co-opt the U.S. military into funding projects they deemed necessary. UNAMA did carry influence as a perceived neutral player in the complicated political playing field of the border provinces.

The successful elections of 2004 and 2005 probably have not received as much recognition as they deserve. Carrying out elections in Afghanistan in the best of times would be difficult, but doing it in the midst of an ongoing insurgency, in a country battered by more than twenty-five years of war, was exceptional. Much of the credit goes to the ability of the various organizations involved to coordinate and integrate their efforts.

Conclusions and Recommendations

By 2008 the situation in EC-East had significantly changed from the fall of 2005. Afghan institutions were making their presence felt, particularly the ANA, which had more troops, an increasing ability to carry out operations, and the support of the Afghan population. After considerable investment by the U.S. in training and equipping the ANP, the police were gradually improving. The IDLG, established in August 2007, was working to improve policy, infrastructure, capacity, and the overall functioning of government at the provincial, district and municipal levels. The IDLG had also brought in several new governors, improving both the administration of the provinces, as well as the outlook of citizens towards their government. At the same time, economic growth in several provinces—notably Nangarhar—was cause for optimism. The trend of increasing Afghan government capacity has changed the dynamics of cooperation—increasingly, U.S. military and civilian officers follow the Afghan lead.

At the same time, the levels of CERP funding were significantly increased. For example, Task Force Bayonet, the brigade command based in Jalalabad, funded roughly $100 million of projects with CERP in 2007, most of which went through the four PRTs in its area of operations (Jalalabad, Asadabad, Mehtar Lam, and Nuristan). The establishment since 2005 of three new PRTs in RC-East—in Wardak, under Turkish leadership, in Logar under Czech leadership, and in Nuristan, under U.S. leadership has allowed for a more "tailored" approach to each of these provinces. Previously, each of these provinces was covered by U.S. PRTs located in adjacent provinces, and was often a secondary effort. The Nuristan PRT in particular has improved the ability to provide development assistance to one of the least developed and most remote Provinces in Afghanistan. Maneuver battalions still play a major role in RC-East. Some areas in Konar Province, particularly the Watapur and Korangal Valleys, still have troops in contact on a regular basis, while sectors of Khost and Paktika Provinces, particularly the border districts, have significant insurgent influence. Some provinces that had only low levels of insurgency in 2004—including parts of Ghazni, Logar, Wardak and Kapisa—now see increased insurgent activity. The maneuver units are needed not only to directly counter the insurgents, but also to support the ANA and ANP, and to allow the Afghan government and the PRTs to operate freely in contested districts. The duties of maneuver units and the PRTs sometimes overlap, particularly in less secure areas, with officers from both involved in CERP projects and supporting the government.

Some provinces appear to be shifting towards the positive end of the security spectrum, so that PRTs (and Afghan government ministries) play an increasing role relative to security forces. An example is Nangarhar province, where in 2004 there were only minimal U.S. and Afghan security forces, and a considerable insurgent presence. By 2008, the ANP, and to a lesser extent the ANA, had the lead on security, and insurgent activity was mostly limited to a few border districts. This allowed the PRT to concentrate on development, spending almost $25 million of CERP funds for projects in 2007, and to focus on working with the governor, the Provincial Council, and tribal leaders. The improved security situation helped a U.S. "special troops battalion," composed of soldiers whose specialties were not combat arms, to succeed as a hybrid combat and development unit.

The need for increased civilian staff at the PRTs and at brigade commands, apparent in 2004 and 2005, remained a problem in 2008. The military has shifted officers to fill these gaps, assigning officers to work on political, development, agricultural, and rule-of-law issues, but the counterinsurgency effort would benefit from more civilian officers with training and experience in these areas. At the same time, UNAMA suffers from being both understaffed and underfunded at both the provincial and regional levels.

On the negative side, various insurgent groups have survived to 2008, including the Taliban, the Haqqani network, al-Qaeda, HIG, and foreign jihadist groups. In some cases, their capabilities have increased (particularly in "asymmetric" warfare such as IEDs and suicide bombings). The resulting low-intensity conflict has had a disproportionate negative impact on development efforts by keeping NGOs out of many areas, diverting money that might be spent on development projects into security, and keeping the U.S. PRTs with a preponderance of military, rather than civilian officers.

Annex IV

Position of RC-East PRTs on the Civil-Military Spectrum, 2004-2005

Each PRT in RC-East, despite similarities in overall organization and strategic goals, was unique in its specific objectives and methods. Each had to adjust to the local conditions—security, economic, geographic, cultural, and political—and adopt its own model, while staying within guidance from higher commands, including the Division command, Brigade command, and the U.S. embassy in Kabul (and, in the case of the New Zealand-led PRT in Bamian, from Wellington).

The security situation in each province was the determining factor for each PRT. Where on the "civil" to "military" spectrum each province was—if kinetic operations predominated, or if reconstruction was the main effort of Coalition forces in the province—determined how the PRT functioned (keeping in mind that no PRT had a combat role to play, other than self-defense). Some provinces, such as Konar, had high threat levels in many areas. This resulted in more emphasis on combat operations, carried out by maneuver units and Special Forces, with the development projects often done in support of these operations. On the other end of the spectrum, PRTs in Bamian and Parwan operated in a much more permissive security environment, and were able to emphasize economic and political development, and reduce (or eliminate) combat operations and patrols.

In very general terms, the security situation improved away from the border with Pakistan; in areas where Hazaras or Tajiks were the predominant ethnic group, or where abundant coalition firepower was available, as in Khost or near Bagram Air Base. Of course, economic and security considerations were closely related, so that in areas with economic growth, including the cities of Jalalabad and Ghazni, the security situation improved as a result. The following describes the resulting PRT "continuum" as it stood in the fall of 2005, from the most challenging security situation (Asadabad, Konar Province and Sharan, Paktika Province) to the most favorable (Bamian, Parwan and Panjshir).

Asadabad

The PRT at Asadabad, in Konar Province across from the FATA's Bajaur Agency, was a case where significant security threats resulted in an emphasis on military operations over development efforts during the years 2004 and 2005. Threats were due to attacks by indigenous insurgent forces, infiltrators from Nuristan Province and Pakistan, and criminal groups involved in smuggling opium, lumber, and jewels. The geographic layout of the province, with the roads often following linear valleys, or with only one route in or out (for example the Pesh Valley road leading to Camp Blessing north of Asadabad) resulted in predictable and unavoidable travel routes, and significant casualties due to IEDs. Beginning in 2005 the Marines were the main maneuver force, operating out of Camp Blessing; they were backed by Special Forces at other bases. By early 2005 smaller ANA units were actively patrolling. The Korangal valley, a very rugged area west of Asadabad, was the site of many contacts, as the insurgents were using it as a staging and supply area (in 2006 a major operation, dubbed "Mountain Lion", was mounted to stabilize the area). By late 2005 the provincial government, with financial support from Kabul, was raising militias at the district levels with the aim of fielding a 2000 man force to counter instability in the province. Because of repeated attacks, some ANP stations were de-facto fire bases, protected with sandbagged towers and heavy machine guns.

The security situation slowed development projects; construction of the road from Jalalabad to Asadabad was repeatedly postponed due to threats, and in at least one case, the death of construction engineers at the hands of insurgents. Movements of the AID representative with the PRT were restricted, and most projects were limited to Asadabad and its surroundings, and to support counterinsurgency operations the Pesh valley. PRT Asadabad was also responsible for the eastern half of Nuristan (with PRT Mehtar Lam responsible for western Nuristan). The focus of efforts there was building rudimentary roads to facilitate future development and to open military lines of communications.

The role of the political officer in Asadabad was particularly important in 2004 and 2005, due to a weak and corrupt provincial government. This led to an eventual housecleaning in early 2005, with the replacement of the governor, NDS chief, and police chief.

Sharan

As described in Annex III concerning Bermel, the security situation in Paktika province made the maneuver battalion predominant relative to the PRT. This was in part due to sheer numbers—the maneuver battalion counted on roughly 700 soldiers, in contrast with 100soldiers manning the PRT. CERP funding levels were roughly equivalent between the maneuver unit and the PRT. AID had signed several million dollars' worth of contracts with the IOM as an implementing partner, but due to security concerns, these projects were on hold, making the CERP funds particularly important.

The first maneuver battalion in Paktika, the 2-27 IN, was on the ground prior to the establishment of the PRT, and built up strong relations with Governor Mangal and other provincial officials and tribes. These strong ties were carried on by the 1-508 IN maneuver battalion. Both battalions pushed units out to the districts, often for extended periods, which the PRT was rarely able to do due to security and manpower restraints. The 1-508 IN established several patrol bases, as well as a permanent base in the south of the province at Waza Khwa. This established a reach the PRT was never able to match. In addition, helicopters were at times made available for operations by the 1-508 IN; such support, which could make a critical difference given the poor road network, was inaccessible to the Sharan PRT—and most other PRTs.

Other factors reduced the effectiveness of the PRT relative to the maneuver battalion. The State Department was not able to place an officer at Sharan until late 2005. Prior to this, the province was covered by the political officer based in Khost. AID was also slow in placing an officer in Sharan. When an AID officer did arrive, an IED attack on a convoy—resulting in the deaths of several Afghan police officers—led to the officer being relocated to Khost. Making matters worse for the PRT, Orgun-E was the previous capital of Paktika, and much political and economic influence remained there. The Special Forces ODB responsible for Paktika was also located in Orgun-E, reducing the chances for synergy with the PRT.

In order to improve coordination with the PRT, the maneuver battalion had assigned a captain as liaison officer. This was an easy arrangement to make, as a small force was assigned to Sharan to help guard the governor's compound. This improved relations, and was also a link for State and AID officers to the commander of the maneuver battalion.

Jalalabad

Given the relatively large population and economic output of Nangarhar Province, its proximity to Pakistan and Peshawar, as well as the considerable poppy cultivation and opium production, Jalalabad was the most important PRT in RC-East. Operations in this province were the most complex, involving the PRT, a substantial USAID effort, Special Forces, Marines, military trainers, and State.

Two AID officers were assigned to the PRT, in part, to handle the heavy workload generated by alternative livelihood programs, and the need to manage sub-contractors such as Development Alternatives International. A USDA officer was assigned to the PRT, advising on agriculture and micro credit (although USDA was hobbled by not having its own funding for projects).

The PRT's presence benefited from a Marine battalion headquartered at JAF, Special Forces, as well as an increasingly strong ANA presence. This helped open access to some of the more difficult districts, particularly in the Spin Ghar range south of Jalalabad, bordering Pakistan, and the heavily tribal districts near the Khyber Pass. The PRT commander, an efficient regular-Army lieutenant colonel, was heavily involved in the complex politics of the province. Several families had traditionally run the province, but there were other poles of power, including the provincial chief of police and the chief of the ABP. The PRT was a moderating influence between the power brokers, extending the influence of the embassy and, more than other PRTs, acting as a de-facto consulate. This influence took several forms—pressing the provincial government to crack down on drug production and corruption; settling disputes between the ANA and the ANP; and reacting to riots that erupted in the spring of 2005, precipitated by an article in Newsweek magazine. While this latter incident damaged security for the short term, overall security was sufficient for development to take precedence over combat operations by the summer of 2005.

Ghazni

During 2004 Ghazni province was relatively peaceful, allowing for freedom of movement by the PRT in most of the province. By the summer of 2005, however, the Taliban was resurgent, making operations more difficult, particularly in the districts bordering Paktika (especially Andar district) and Zabol Provinces. The Ghazni PRT also covered Wardak Province, a difficult assignment given the distances and poor roads in that province. The PRT benefited from sharing its base with an army maneuver battalion, easing its access to less secure parts of the province. Interestingly, the Afghan Highway Police was a significant factor in provincial security, not only by keeping the Kabul to Kandahar ring road open, but also by serving as the governor's private militia.

The political and AID officers shared strong working relations with Governor Assadullah Khalid, a young and vigorous official with strong ties to both the Northern Alliance and President Karzai. This relationship in some ways engendered a textbook form of what a PRT political officer may hope to achieve —improving the efficiency of the provincial government; shaming the governor into doing the right thing; acting as an honest broker (with a mixed Tajik, Hazara, and Pashtun population, politicians from these various groups at times caused problems for their own ends); and explaining USG programs and policies.

An additional U.S. maneuver battalion was assigned to Ghazni and Wardak Provinces for the September 2005 provincial elections. This brought a significant increase in security to areas that had previously had only occasional coalition presence. An opportunity was missed, however, by not assigning a State officer to this temporary deployment.

Mehtar Lam

Laghman Province had been fairly quiet following the 2001 overthrow of the Taliban, with insurgent activity occurring mostly in two northern districts. The Mehtar Lam PRT also covered western Nuristan province. The PRT initially shared a base with a Marine company, which aggressively patrolled in the province. In part, due to the Marine's presence, the PRT was able to make rapid progress in several areas. In coordination with the provincial government, DDR was effective in demobilizing several militia groups and bringing in Taliban members. The 2005 parliamentary elections were used as leverage against several warlords, who were forced to at least partially disarm before becoming eligible as candidates.

In general, the combined PRT/Marine presence seemed to give confidence to the local government, headed by the reasonably competent Governor Shah Mahmood Safi. Several development projects—including roads in the Alishang Valley—were begun. The civilian presence at Mehtar Lam was limited at first, with Jalalabad-based State and AID officers providing coverage when possible. The AID presence was primarily a counternarcotics effort to promote alternative livelihoods, and construct the road linking Mehtar Lam with Route 1. By late 2005 a State officer had been permanently assigned to the PRT.

Bamian

Within RC-East, the Bamian PRT was unique for several reasons. Although it was an OEF PRT, it was commanded and staffed by New Zealand soldiers. They brought their own doctrine to the field, including a "softer" approach emphasizing reconstruction and community relations over combat operations. The population in Bamian Province is predominantly of the Hazara ethnic group, who are mostly Shiite Muslims. As a result, the Taliban and other insurgents groups had difficulties operating in Bamian, and the security situation was permissive. This allowed the PRT to operate without the support of a maneuver battalion, relying instead on their limited combat capabilities (rarely, if ever used) and the presence of Afghan security forces. The Hazara have historically been an underclass in Afghanistan, and have received limited development assistance over the years. The PRT's development projects therefore made a disproportionately large impact. The PRT worked closely with Governor Habiba Sarobi, Afghanistan's only woman governor, supporting her in struggles against corrupt government and police officials. This PRT had an unusually large proportion of medics, and made good use of MEDCAPs throughout the province. Officers from USAID, State and USDA were posted to the PRT, making their agencies resources available in support of the New Zealand effort.

In contrast to the situation in Bermel, Bamian was a case where the PRT was able to lead, without any maneuver battalion support to speak of. The security situation was good enough that the focus was almost entirely on reconstruction work and development of the provincial government.

Panjshir

The Panjshir PRT was also unique among OEF PRTs, with a State Department officer designated as the commander instead of a military officer. Only a minimal number of soldiers were assigned to the PRT, and its focus was on political and economic development. This arrangement was made possible by the special conditions in the Panjshir Valley—a receptive Tajik population, a provincial government willing to assure the PRT's security, and the difficulty the Taliban or other insurgent groups had operating in Panjshir. The Panjshir model had significant benefits—a smaller footprint, cheaper costs, and reliance on local capabilities. However, this model may be difficult to replicate in areas where the security situation is more fluid.

Notes

Foreword

[1] The American Academy of Diplomacy, *A Foreign Affairs Budget for the Future*, 2008.
[2] Ronald E. Neumann, *The Other War: Winning and Losing in Afghanistan* (Washington, D.C.: Potomac Books, 2009), 204–5.

Chapter 1

[1] Barnett Rubin, *The Fragmentation of Afghanistan: State Formation and Collapse in the International System*, 2nd ed. (New Haven: Yale University Press, 2002), 143.
[2] U.S. Government, represented by the Secretary of the Army, *Afghanistan: A Country Study*, 1986.
[3] Martin Ewans, *Afghanistan: A Short History of Its People and Politics* (New York: HarperCollins Publishers, 2002), 235.
[4] U.S. Government, *Afghanistan: A Country Study*, 343.
[5] Ralph H. Magnus and Eden Naby, *Afghanistan: Mullah, Marx, and Mujahid* (Westview Press, 2002), 147.
[6] Rubin, *Fragmentation of Afghanistan*, 38.
[7] Magnus, Mullah, Marx and Mujahid, 75.
[8] United Nations Development Programme, *National Human Development Report: Afghanistan*, ed. Shahrbanou Tadjbakhsh (Islamabad: Army Press, 2004). http://hdr.undp.org/en/reports/national/asiathe pacific/afghanistan/Afghanistan_2004_en.pdf

Chapter 2

[9] International Monetary Fund, *IMF Country Report No. 08/153 Afghanistan National Development Strategy* (Washington D.C.: IMF Publication Services, 2008). http://www.imf.org/external/pubs/ft/scr/2008/cr08153.pdf

10. For a general discussion, see "Counterinsurgency in Eastern Afghanistan" by the author, in the compendium by the Council for Emerging National Security Affairs, "Counter Insurgency and Promoting Democracy," Manolis Priniotakis, editor, 2007
11. U.S Army Brigades in Afghanistan had between 5,000 and 7,000 personnel in them, often including smaller units temporarily attached to the brigade for specific tasks such as logistics or aviation support.
12. The U.S. Army and U.S. Marine Corps, *Counterinsurgency Field Manual* (Chicago: University of Chicago Press, 2007), Glossary 5, provides this working definition of COIN: "*insurgency* is an organized movement aimed at the overthrow of a constituted government through the use of subversion and armed conflict. Stated another way, an insurgency is an organized, protracted politico-military struggle designed to weaken the control and legitimacy of an established government, occupying power, or other political authority while increasing insurgent control. *Counterinsurgency* is military, paramilitary, political, economic, psychological, and civic actions taken by a government to defeat insurgency." In contrast, counterterrorism includes the tactics and strategies governments use to attack terrorist groups, and prevent terrorist acts. Pg. 1-1, ibid
13. "Progress Towards Stability and Security in Afghanistan," January 2009 Report to Congress. http://www.defense,gov/pubs/october_1230_final.pdf pg 7
14. Sebastien Trives, "Roots of the Insurgency in the Southeast," in *Decoding the New Taliban: Insights from the Afghan Field*," ed. Antonio Giustozzi (Colombia University Press, 2009), 93.
15. Jeffery Dressler, "The Haqqani Network: From Pakistan to Afghanistan," in *Institute for the Study of War* (October 2010), 20. http://www.understandingwar.org. This monograph by Dressler looks at the origins, ideology, and operations of the Haqqani network.

Chapter 4

16. Interview with the author, Fall 2011, Washington DC.
17. Gradizi, Hussman, and Turabi explain corruption in Afghanistan this way: "Contemporary Afghan society has its own understanding of what constitutes corruption, which is often directly based on experience. It includes bribery, extortion, nepotism, co-optation of power holders, and outright theft from state coffers, but also other socially unacceptable practices such as exorbitant salaries for internationally paid staff."
Manija Gradizi, Karen Hussmann, and Yama Turabi, "Corrupting the State or State-Crafted Corruption? Exploring the Nexus between Corruption and Subnational Governance," in *Afghanistan Research and Evalu-*

ation Unit (June 2010). http://areu.org.af/EditionDetails.aspx?EditionId=356&ContentId=7&Lang=en-US

Chapter 5

[18] Sarah Lister and Hamish Nixon, "The Place of the Province in Afghanistan's Subnational Governance," in *Rebuilding Afghanistan*, ed. Robert Rotberg (Washington, DC: Brooking Institution Press, 2007).

[19] Robert Kemp, "Civil-Military Cooperation as a Function of Security, Eastern Afghanistan, 2004-2005," in *Campaigning* (Summer 2008), 32-42. www.jfsc.ndu.edu/ schools_programs/jcws/Publications/Campaigning_Journal_Summer_2008.pdf.

[20] Hamish Nixon, "Subnational State Building in Afghanistan," *Afghanistan Research and Evaluation Unit Synthesis Paper Series* (April 2008), 20.

[21] Afghanistan National Development Strategy website, Strategy Paper on Launching of the Independent Directorate for Local Governance.<www.ands. gov.af>.

[22] Constitution of the Islamic Republic of Afghanistan, Article 137. http://www.servat.unibe.ch/icl/af00000_.html Note: there are variations in English versions (see, for example, the slightly different wording of Article 137 at the Afghan Embassy website: .http://www.embassyofafghanistan.org/document/the-constitution-of-the-islamic-republic-of-afghanistan

[23] Robert Rotberg, *Building a New Afghanistan* (Brookings Institution Press, 2007), pg. 207.

[24] *Counterinsurgency Field Manual*, Section 6-1.

[25] Interview with the author, summer 2012, Washington DC.

Chapter 6

[26] United States Government Accountability Office, "Securing, Stabilizing, and Reconstructing Afghanistan," *Report to Congressional Committees* 07-801SP (May 2007). http://www.gao.gov/products/GAO-07-801SP pg. 28.

[27] USAID, "USAID Afghanistan Strategy,"Document 1. http://pdf.usaid.gov/pdf_docs/pdac1740.pdf pg. 1.

[28] USAID, "USAID Assistance to Afghanistan 2002-2008,"http://pdf.usaid.gov/pdf_docs/pdacp518.pdf pg.1.

[29] Majority Staff Report for U.S. Senate Committee on Foreign Relations, S. Prt. 112-21 *Evaluating U.S. Foreign Assistance to Afghanistan*, (Washington D.C.: U.S. Government Printing Office, 2011), 15.http://www.foreign.senate.gov/publications/?c=112&type=committee_print pg. 15.

[30] Center for Army Lessons Learned, *Commander's Emergency Response Program: Handbook*. http://ublishintelligence.net/ufouo-commander%E2%80%99s-emergency-response-program-cerp-handbook/ pg.i.

[31] United States Government Accountability Office, "Military Operations: Actions Needed to Improve Oversight and Interagency Coordination for the Commander's Emergency Response Program in Afghanistan," *Report to Congressional Committees* 09-615 (May 2009). http://www.gao.gov/new.items/d09615.pdf pg. 1.

[32] Ibid., 9.

[33] Mark W. Lee, "The Commander's Emergency Response Program: Synergistic Results Through Training," in *Army Sustainment*, May-June 2010. http://www.almc.army.mil/alog/issues/May-June10/synergy_thrutrain.html pg.2.

[34] USAID, *Increasing Access to Quality Education and Sustainable Learning Environments*. http://afghanistan.usaid.gov/en/programs/education.

[35] The World Bank, *Education in Afghanistan*, www.worldbank.org.af/wbsite/external/countries/southasia.

[36] Performance Based Governor's Fund, *Handbook*, http://pbgf.gov.af/file.php?id=19&code=3693eal

[37] David K. Spencer, "Afghanistan's Nangarhar Inc: A Model for Interagency Success," *Military Review* 89, no. 4 (2009). Robert Kemp, "Counterinsurgency in Nangarhar Province, Eastern Afghanistan, 2004-2008," *Military Review* 90, no. 6 (2010).

[38] The Asia Foundation, *Afghanistan in 2008: A Survey of the Afghan People*, http://asiafoundation.org/publications/pdf/418.pg.5

[39] David Kilcullen, *The Accidental Guerrilla: Fighting Small Wars in the Midst of a Large One* (New York: Oxford, 2009), 71.

[40] Ibid., 107.

[41] Carter Malkasian and Gerald Meyerle, *Provincial Reconstruction Teams: How Do We Know They Work?* (Carlisle: Strategic Studies Institute: 2009), viii.

[42] Wilton Park Conference 1022, "Winning 'Hearts and Minds' in Afghanistan: Assessing the Effectiveness of Development Aid in COIN Operations" (March 2010). https://wikis.uit.tyfts.edu/confluence/download/attachments/34085577/WP1022.pdf?version=1&modificationDate=1270215996000, pg.2

[43] Andrew Wilder, "Money Can't Buy America Love," *Foreign Policy* (December 1, 2009).

[44] Majority Staff Report S. Prt. 112-21, 14.

[45] David Rodriguez, "Leaving Afghanistan to the Afghans," *Foreign Affairs* (September-October 2011), 50.

Chapter 7

[46] See, for example: Kilkullen, *Accidental Guerrilla*, and Seth Jones, *In the*

Notes   211

Graveyard of Empires: America's War in Afghanistan, W.W. Norton and Company, 2009.

47 This end-state is taken from a widely circulated CFC-A powerpoint slide. For an example of this slide, see Cameron Sellers, *Provincial Reconstruction Teams: Improving Effectiveness* (Monterey: Naval Postgraduate School, September 2007), pg. 76.

48 Pat Donahue and Michael Fenzel, "Combating a Modern Insurgency: Combined Task Force Devil in Afghanistan" in *Military Review* (March 2008).

49 Ibid.

50 Colonel William Ostland, U.S. Army, "Tactical Leader Lessons Learned in Afghanistan: Operation Enduring Freedom VIII" in *Military Review* (July-August 2009).

51 Ibid.

52 For an excellent description of this long-running battle, see Sebastian Junger, *War*, Hachette Book Group, 2010; and Sebastian Junger and Tim Hetherington, *Restrepo*, a film distributed by National Geographic Entertainment, 2010.

53 For a discussion of information operations, see: Arturo Munoz, *U.S. Military Information Operations in Afghanistan: Effectiveness of Psychological Operations 2001–2010* (Rand National Defense Research Institute, 2012). http://www.rand.org/content/dam/rand/pubs/monographs/2012/RAND_MG1060.pdf

Chapter 8

54 Stanley McChrystal, "Commander's Initial Assessment" from Commander, NATO International Security Assistance Force, Afghanistan and U.S. Forces, Afghanistan, published by *The Washington Post* (September 21, 2009). http://articles.washingtonpost.com/2009-09-21/news/36848328_1_international-security-assistance-force-civilian-casualties-review-plans. *Counterinsurgency Field Manual.*

55 The U.S. Army and U.S. Marine Corps, *Counterinsurgency Field Manual* (Chicago: University of Chicago Press, 2007), pg 1-113

56 Robert Kemp, "Local Governance and COIN, in Eastern Afghanistan, 2004-2008," in *Military Review* (November–December 2010), 34.

57 The U.S. Army and U.S. Marine Corps, *Counterinsurgency Field Manual* (Chicago: University of Chicago Press, 2007), p 2-1.

58 Ostland, "Tactical Leader Lessons."

59 Michael T Flynn, Maj. Gen., U.S. Army, Capt. Matt Pottinger, U.S. Marine Corps, and Paul D. Batchelor, Defense Intelligence Agency,„ *Fixing*

Intel: A Blueprint for Making Intelligence Relevant in Afghanistan, Center for New American Security (January 2010). http://www.cnas.org/files/documents/publictions/AfghanIntel_Flynn_Jan2010_code507_voices.pdf

[60] David Kilcullen, *The Accidental Guerilla*, (New York: Oxford University Press, 2009), p 60.

[61] Kilcullen, *Accidental Guerilla*, p. 298.

[62] The U.S. Army and U.S. Marine Corps, *Counterinsurgency Field Manual*, pp 2–12.

[63] The U.S. Army and U.S. Marine Corps, *Counterinsurgency Field Manual*, pp 1–26.

Chapter 9

[64] Telephone interview with the author, Fall 2011.

[65] U.S. Customs and Border Protection, "CBP Personnel Advising on Afghanistan Border Security Strategy" in *Frontline* (Summer 2009), 34. http://nemo.cbp.gov/opa/frontline/summer_09_fl.pdf

[66] Seth G. Jones and C. Christine Fair, *Counterinsurgency in Pakistan*, Rand National Security Research Division, 2010. Congressional Research Service, "Islamic Militancy in the Pakistan-Afghanistan Border Region and U.S. Policy," November 2008. Shuja Nawaz, *FATA—A Most Dangerous Place: Meeting the Challenge of Militancy and Terror in the Federally Administered Tribal Areas of Pakistan* (Washington: Center for Strategic and International Studies, January 2009), in *Center for Strategic and International Studies* (January 2009). International Crisis Group, "Pakistan's Tribal Areas: Appeasing the Militants" in *Asia Report* no.125 (December 2006). http://www.crisisgroup.org/en/regions/asia/south-asia/pakistan/125-pakistans-tribal-areas-appeasing-the-militants.aspx

[67] North Atlantic Treaty Organization, Topic: "NATO's Relations with Pakistan—Cooperation on Afghanistan" on NATO website. http://www.nato.int/cps/en/SID-9765B1A7-21D9EDD4/natolive/topics_50071.htm

[68] Conversations between the author and various Afghan governors, 2004 -5.

Chapter 10

[69] United Nations Office on Drugs and Crime and Government of Afghanistan Ministry of Counter Narcotics, "Afghanistan Opium Survey, Executive Survey," August 2008. http://www.unodc.org/documents/publications/Afghanistan_Opium_Survey_2008.pdf

[70] Observations by the author.

[71] Interview by author of former U.S. ambassador to Afghanistan, Spring 2012.

[72] David Mansfield, "Between a Rock and a Hard Place: Counter-narcotics efforts and their effects in Nangarhar and Helmand in the 2010–2011 Growing Season," *Afghanistan Research and Evaluation Unit* (October 2011). http://www.areu.org.af/Uploads/EditionPdfs/1128E-Between%20a%20 Rock%20and%20a%20Hard%20Place-CS-2011.pdf. See VandaFelbab-Brown, *Shooting Up: Counterinsurgency and the War on Drugs* (Washington D.C.: Brookings Institution Press, 2010) for discussions of unintended consequences of counternarcotics efforts, and sustainability.

Chapter 11

[73] Neamatollah Nojumi, *The Rise of the Taliban in Afghanistan* (Palgrave, 2002), 129.
[74] UNAMA, *Suicide Attacks in Afghanistan 2001–2007*(Kabul: UNAMA, 2007), 3.http://www.securitycouncilreport.org/atf/cf/%7B65BFCF9B-6D27-4E9C-8CD3-CF6E4FF9%7D/Afgh%202007SuicideAttacks.pdf
[75] Ibid., 38.
[76] Hanif Atmar, Interview by David Loyn, *Newsnight*, BBC, January 12, 2008.

Chapter 12

[77] Georgetown student Matthew Giebler, in his senior thesis "The Time of the Men with Guns: The Local Security Option in Afghanistan, 2001–2012," Georgetown University, 2012, makes the following observations on this issue: Local security forces in Afghanistan tended to be successful when they met the following criteria: (1) local security programs were implemented jointly by ISAF and the Afghan government; (2) traditional institutions were involved and had meaningful roles; (3) recruits were thoroughly vetted by the Afghan government with input from local elder councils; (4) local security force members were trained by ISAF or Afghan trainers, specifically by Special Operations Forces (SOF), in practical operations as well as legal, ethical, and human rights concepts; (5) local security forces were both ethnically and locally representative of the communities they protected; (6) local security forces were established after the 2009 ISAF troop surge and shift toward counterinsurgency strategy; and (7) individual units of local security forces were small in scope, allowing for adaptability to local conditions.

The most significant factor that contributed to the failure of local security programs was the involvement of local warlords or powerbrokers who exploited the support of international actors and the Afghan government to promote their own interests.

[78] Dr. Arturo Munoz, in his perceptive chapter "A Long Overdue Adaptation to the Afghan Environment" in *The Long Shadow of 9/11*, ed. Brian Michael Jenkins and John Godges (Rand Corporation, 2011), 33-34.http://www.rand.org/pubs/monographs/MG1107.html), noted that "U.S. attempts to develop local defense forces illustrate the difficulty of balancing local and national priorities in Afghanistan. After 2001, as the Taliban turned to guerrilla war, various tribal communities formed *arbakai* on their own to combat them. This is what any good counterinsurgency campaign is looking for and wants to support: local people willing to fight the insurgents. In 2009, to stimulate that process, U.S. General Stanley McChrystal backed the creation of the Local Defense Initiative (LDI). However, U.S. Ambassador Karl Eikenberry opposed it, fearing that local forces would inevitably engage in traditional feuding or support warlords. Consequently, the LDI term was abandoned in favor of Village Stability Operations (VSO). Based on assessments of the positive impact of VSO, U.S. General David Petraeus today strongly supports the program, and a systematic effort organized by the Combined Forces Special Operations Component Command–Afghanistan is underway to expand the number of participating villages on an expedited basis.

"However, the Karzai administration has expressed concern over foreigners sponsoring local forces and the potential proliferation of uncontrolled militias. In August 2010, his administration inaugurated its own, more centralized program, the Afghan Local Police (ALP), focusing on recruitment and training of local men to become uniformed, salaried policemen controlled by the district or provincial chief of police, under the Afghan Ministry of Interior. To avoid the potential anomaly of two parallel programs, Petraeus signed on to the ALP. The mutually agreed upon compromise calls for the security elements of VSO to be absorbed by the ALP; that is, members of VSO local defense forces eventually will become ALP policemen. Afghan and U.S. officials currently refer to all local forces as ALP, but it remains to be seen whether they will function more as community-based civilian defense forces or as uniformed policemen."

[79] For a detailed discussion of metrics in counterinsurgency, see Ben Connable, *Embracing the Fog of War: Assessment and Metrics in Counterinsurgency* (Rand Corporation, 2012).

Chapter 13

[80] Conversation with Afghan government official, 2007, Kabul.

[81] Interview with the author, January 2012, Washington DC.

[82] Interview with the author, Fall 2011, Washington DC

[83] For more background on civilian-military relations, the COIN Manual outlines some best practices as well as some case studies. The book *Counterinsurgency on the Ground in Afghanistan,* edited by Jerry Meyerle, Megan Katt and Jim Gavrilis, CNA, November 2010, has several insightful vignettes that touch on civ-mil cooperation. While dealing with events in Helmand Province, Carter Malkasian's excellent book *War Comes to Garmser* (New York: Oxford University Press, 2013) also addresses civ-mil cooperation.

[84] http://web.worldbank.org/WBSITE/EXTERNAL/COUNTRIES/SOUTHASIAEXT/ADGHANISTANEXTN/0_menuPK:305990-pagePK:141159-piPK:141110-theSitePK:141110-theSitePK:305985.00.htm.
This World Bank study takes an in-depth look at Afghanistan's macroeconomic and financial situation. It also projects future economic trends, including models of what the economy might look like should there be a drastic reduction in foreign assistance.

ANNEX I

[85] Independent Directorate of Local Governance, "District Delivery Program Secretariat: Support to District Delivery Program," Draft version 2.3. http://info.publicintelligence.net/AfghanDistrictDeliveryPlanSecretariat.pdf.

[86] Department of State, "Afghanistan and Pakistan Regional Stabilization Plan," *Office of the Special Representative for Afghanistan and Pakistan,* Feb. 2010. http://www.state.gov/documents/organization/135728.pdf

[87] Independent Directorate of Local Governance, "District Delivery Program as of March 10 2010 Briefing," https"//www.cimicweb.org/Documents/PRT%20CONFERENCE%202010/District%20Delivery%20Program_corrected%20%5BCompatibiity%Mode%5D.pdf

[88] USAID, "Independent Directorate of Local Governance: District Delivery Program," August 2010–February 2013.http://www.usaid.gov/node/51831

[89] This included, on the military side, the Afghan National Military Strategy, ISAF OPLAN 38302, and ISAF Joint Command (IJC) OPORD OMID 1390. On the civilian or civilian-military side, it included the USG's "Integrated Civ-Mil Campaign Plan," the Afghan National Development Strategy (ANDS), the newly developed Sub-National Governance Policy, and United Nations Assistance Mission in Afghanistan (UNAMA) programs for local governance.

[90] The most relevant being the Ministries of Agriculture, Irrigation and Livestock (MAIL); Interior; Education; Justice; Public Health, and Rural Rehabilitation and Development (MRRD).

[91] Through CIDA and DIFD, respectively.

[92] The MRRD, Ministry of Education, Public Health, MAIL, the Attorney General's Office, Afghan Civil Service Institute, Supreme Court, as well as some representatives of the international community

[93] According to a USAID website: "Increased U.S. involvement in crisis, conflict, and post-conflict settings has created a demand for tools to identify and diminish the causes of instability. Traditional civilian and military tools have not been effective in unstable areas because the conditions are dramatically different from normal development environments. These areas are often insecure, economically devastated, and have ineffective or non-existent government institutions. Responding to this need, the Office of Civilian-Military Cooperation (CMC), along with USAID's Office of Transition Initiatives (OTI) and the Counterinsurgency Training Center in Kabul, Afghanistan, created the District Stability Framework (DSF). The DSF is a simple, standardized, four-part assessment and planning tool." (USAID, "District Stability Framework)" http://www.usaid.gov/work-usaid/partnership-opportunities/us-military/training/district-stability-frameworkupdated February 08, 2013).

[94] According to USAID documents, "Funding Stream 1 provides on-budget partial salary support, hazard pay, and operational and maintenance funds for district officials and offices in key sectors (administration, health, justice, agriculture, and education) via the Afghan budgetary system. Funding Stream 2 aligns traditional USAID development and Afghan government programs to provide services as prioritized by district officials and community representatives. Funding Stream 3 is U.S. Military funds used to finance small-scale district government infrastructure related to service delivery. During its second year, DDP will seek to strengthen fiscal flows and accountability mechanisms from the center, provinces and districts and to improve basic service delivery at the district level in collaboration with key ministries." USAID, "Independent Directorate of Local Governance: District Delivery Program," August 2010–February 2013.

[95] This was in addition to the Afghan National Development Plan and the Sub-National Governance Policy.

[96] According to USAID documents, ASOP "aims to strengthen security and peace, improve the effectiveness and responsiveness of service delivery, and build local governance through the revival of traditional practices of collective decision-making, community solidarity, and promoting cooperation and partnership with the government. The program is designed to put in place mechanisms to ensure ongoing communication and collaboration between the government and communities through the creation of community councils at the district level." USAID, *Afghanistan*

Social Outreach Program (ASOP) District Community Council's Management and Operation Training Manual. (AECOM International Development, June 2011), pg 19. http://pdf.usaid.gov/pdf_docs/pnady818.pdf. See also: AID's "Afghanistan Social Outreach Program: Final Report" http://pdf.usaid.gov/pdf_docs/pdact585.pdf

[97] According to UNDP documents, NABDP "aims to promote recovery and longer term development in Afghanistan while building the government's capacity to lead and coordinate participatory approaches to development." This included "the capacity building of District Development Assemblies (DDA), will help promote the partnership between the public and private sector" and "Develop rural development infrastructure to promote the creation of rural incomes, employment and economic opportunities" which potentially overlapped with DDP. United Nations Development Program, "National Area-Based Development Programme," (NABD Factsheet. May 2011). http://www.undp.org.af/Projects/Report2011/nabdp/Project-ANBDP-May2011-factsheet.pdf

[98] USAID, "Fact Sheet: Local Governance and Community Development (LGCD)," June 2011. http://www.usaid.gov/sites/default/files/documents/1871/Fact%20sheet%20LGCD%20June%202011.pdf

[99] Randy George and Dante Paradiso, "Does the Afghan War Need a CEO? The Case for a Wartime Chief Executive Officer: Fixing the Interagency Quagmire in Afghanistan" in *Foreign Affairs*(June 21, 2011) http://www.foreignaffairs.com/discussions/roundtables/does-the-afghan-war-need-a-ceo

[100] Asia Foundation. *Afghanistan 2011: A Survey of the Afghan People*. ed. Ruth Rennie (Kabul: AINA Media, 2011). http://asiafoundation.org/resources/pdfs/TAF2011AGSurvey.pdf

[101] The Afghan NSC had only limited impact on DDP coordination.

[102] Independent Directorate of Local Governance, "District Delivery Program: Initial Lessons Learned" (April, 2010). http://publicintelligence.net/government-of-islamic-republic-of-afghanistan-district-development-program-lessons-learned

[103] Discussion with the author by IDLG official, Washington DC, 2012.

[104] Douglas Saltmarshe and Abhilash Medhi, "Local Governance in Afghanistan: A View from the Ground," *Afghanistan Research and Evaluation Unit* (June 2011). http://www.areu.org.af/EditionDetails.aspx?EditionId=542&ParentId=7&ContentId=7&Lang=en-US

[105] Mission of Afghanistan to the United Nations, "Effective Public Administration Vital to Deliver Services to Afghan Citizens, says World Bank report" (June 10, 2008). http://www.afghanistan-un.org/2008/06/effective-public-administration-vital-to-deliver-services-to-afghan-citizens-says-world-bank-report

[106] Interview by author Washington DC, 2012.

Annex II

[107] Interview with former U.S. ambassador, summer 2012.
[108] Jerry Meyerle, Megan Katt, Jim Gavrilis, *Counterinsurgency on the Ground in Afghanistan* (CNA Strategic Studies, 2010).http://www.cna.org/research/2010/counterinsurgency-ground-afghanistan
[109] Mohammad Yousaf and Mark Adkin, *The Battle for Afghanistan* (Pen and Sword Books, 2007).

Index

101st Airborne Division 121, 122
173rd 3Airborne Brigade 72, 100
2nd Battalion, 27th Infantry 37

Afghan Border Police (ABP) 72, 77, 99, 100, 103, 113, 115, 181, 182, 193, 202
Afghan Local Police (ALP) 143, 174, 214
Afghan Militia Force (AMF) 77, 100, 176, 180, 182
Afghan National Army (ANA) 72, 73, 75, 77, 79, 100–101, 102, 113–14, 122, 137, 139, 143, 153, 157, 174, 176, 179, 180–82, 186, 188, 191, 195–96, 200, 202–3
Afghan National Development Strategy (ANDS) 10, 17, 40, 49, 55, 61
Afghan National Police (ANP) 72, 77, –8079, 92, 99, 100, 102, 113–15, 137, 143, 174, 176, 179, 181, 182, 186, 191, 192, 193, 195, 196, 200, 203
Afghan National Security Forces (ANSF) 69, 70, 71, 74, 76, 135, 136, 143, 145, 146, 166, 173
Afghan Social Outreach Program (ASOP) 168
Afghanistan Reconstruction Group (ARG) 54, 121, 122
Afghanistan Vouchers for Increased Productive Agriculture (AVIPA) 168
Agricultural Development Teams, (ADTs) 52, 155
al-Qaeda 2, 18, 24, 25, 26, 128, 129, 136, 155, 177, 197
alberkai 77, 78, 101, 179, 186
Asadabad 71, 73, 75, 196, 200, 201
Attorney General's Office 163, 216

Bajaur Agency 132, 200
Bamian Province 4, 15, 37, 88, 150, 204, 205
Barno, LTG David 28, 70
Bermel 192–93
Border Coordination Centers (BCCs) 105, 114
Border Management Task Force (BMTF) 103, 104
Brussels 54, 86, 141

Camp Blessing 200
CENTCOM 51, 70
Civil Service Commission 163
Civilian Affairs Team–Alpha (CAT-A) 177, 179
Civil-Military Operations Center (CMOC) 177, 178
CJTF-76 71

Index

Combined Forces Command–Afghanistan 18, 70
Combined Joint Special Operations Task Force 70
Combined Security Transition Command-Afghanistan (CSTC-A) 70
Commander's Emergency Response Program (CERP) 47–49, 51, 58, 61-64, 71–74, 76, 85, 86, 92, 95, 103, 115, 116, 120, 137, 167, 168, 177, 179, 182, 184, 194, 196, 197, 201
CTF Devil 71–72

Daikundi 4, 77, 91
Deobandi 9, 127, 128
Disarmament, Demobilization, and Reintegration (DDR) 182, 204
Disbandment of Illegal Armed Groups (DIAG) 101, 182
District Community Councils 166
District Support Teams (DSTs) 95, 164, 165, 166, 168, 170, 172, 173
Drug Enforcement Agency (DEA) 87, 118
Durand Line 11 192

Eikenberry, Karl 70, 143, 172, 214

Federally Administered Tribal Areas (FATA) 6, 24, 26, 72, 78, 96, 101, 105, 113, 122, 123, 128, 129, 132, 134, 174, 175, 192, 200
Frontier Corps 78, 105, 134, 141, 176

Gardez 4, 19, 29, 71, 131, 150, 181, 184, 189, 194, 195
Ghazni 20, 26, 32, 33, 35, 46, 52, 57, 60, 67, 69, 70, 72, 76, 87, 90, 138, 147, 150, 185, 197, 200, 203, 204

Good Performers Initiative 53
Haqqani network 19, 38, 129, 136, 140, 175, 197
Hazara 5-8, 15, 26, 33, 87, 88, 91, 140, 146, 150, 200, 203, 204, 205
Helmand Province 37, 41, 94, 161, 169, 170, 174
Hezb-e Islami Khalis (HIK) 117
Hezb-e- Islami Gulbuddin (HIG) 23, 26, 117, 127, 129, 136, 140, 197
Holbrooke, Richard 66, 91, 92, 94

Improvised explosive devices (IEDs) 3, 23, 25, 26, 57, 70, 101, 113, 114, 176, 178, 183, 184, 197
Independent Directorate of Local Governance (IDLG) 39, 40, 41, 42, 49, 53, 94, 145, 161-172, 195
Integrated Civil-Military Action Group 54
Interagency Provincial Affairs 163
International Narcotics and Law Enforcement Bureau (INL) 53, 87, 118, 120
International Organization for Migration (IOM) 50, 183, 201
International Security Assistance Force (ISAF) 28, 34, 56, 70, 71, 86, 88, 103, 104, 105, 131, 135, 153, 161, 162, 164, 171–74
Iran 2, 5, 149, 150
Islam 5, 8, 24,117, 127-134, 143, 146, 151, 153

Jalalabad xiv, 4, 24, 28, 29, 38, 45, 57, 70. 71, 72, 73, 75, 76, 77, 100, 104, 112–25, 138, 151, 153, 194, 200, 202–3.
Jamaat-e-Islami 127, 129
Joint Coordination Monitoring Board 54

Kandahar Province 2, 116, 121, 128, 146, 161, 169, 174
Kapisa Province 67, 91, 196
Karzai, President Hamid 32, 36, 39, 40, 41, 106, 114, 116, 136, 142, 154, 163, 203
Key Terrain Districts 66, 165
Khalid, Governor Assadullah 203
Khyber Pass 48, 74, 104, 112, 119, 150, 202
Konar Province 2, 13, 24, 41, 69, 70, 76, 87, 101, 191, 196, 200
Korangal Valley 24, 74, 75, 196, 200, 201
Kuchis 7, 33, 87
Kurram Agency 100, 122, 123, 132, 175

Laghman Province 41, 72, 74, 79, 81, 94, 204
lines of communications 142, 201
Logar Province 20, 32, 67, 69, 90, 178, 189, 196

madrassa 52, 90, 128, 129, 131, 132–133, 177, 188
Mangal, Governor Mohammed Gulab 32, 41, 94, 192, 201
McChrystal, Gen. Stanley 171, 214
Mehtar Lam 73, 196, 201, 204
meshrano jirga 11, 39
Ministry of Agriculture, Irrigation and Livestock (MAIL) 49
Ministry of Border and Tribal Affairs 49
Ministry of Education 49, 53, 144, 216
Ministry of Finance 162, 167, 169, 172
Ministry of Public Health 49
Ministry of Rural Rehabilitation and Development (MRRD) 49, 169, 175

Ministry of Women's Affairs 49
Ministry of Interior (MOI) 39, 171, 174, 178

National Directorate for Security (NDS) 77, 145
National Solidarity Program 49, 88, 168
NATO 1, 28, 48, 53, 67, 70, 86, 105, 113, 115, 141, 155, 161
New Zealand 88, 199, 204, 205
NGOs, xv, xvii, 28, 44, 51, 55, 56, 60, 65, 76, 96, 140, 183, 187, 188, 197
North West Frontier Province (NWFP) 11, 78, 128, 129, 134, 141
Nuristan Province 4, 24, 37, 51, 69, 72, 73, 74, 77, 91, 102, 103, 114, 123, 139, 196
Nuristanis 6, 8, 89, 129, 196

Office of the Coordinator for Reconstruction and Stabilization 54
Operation Enduring Freedom (OEF) 18, 70, 72, 177, 187, 204, 205
Orgun-E 76, 100, 193, 202
Overseas Humanitarian, Disaster, and Civic Aid (OHDACA) 184

Pakistan x, xv, xvii, 1, 2, 4, 5, 6, 7, 11, 15, 23, 24, 25, 26, 27, 31, 48, 52, 57, 61, 66, 67, 69, 70, 71, 72, 73, 74, 78, 89, 90, 91, 92, 99–110, 112, 113, 114, 115, 116, 117, 122, 127–34, 135, 140, 141, 145, 149, 150, 153, 156, 163, 174, 175, 176, 178, 180
PAKMIL 26, 67, 78, 105, 133, 134, 141,

Paktia Province 2, 7, 19, 23, 24, 25, 24, 26, 32, 130, 132, 139, 157, 188, 193, 194,

Paktika Province 4, 12, 19, 23, 24, 25, 26, 32, 33, 37, 38, 69, 77, 80, 91, 94, 100, 101, 102, 109, 132, 139, 176, 192, 193, 194, 196, 200, 201,

Panjshir 69, 87, 191, 200, 205

Performance-Based Governor's Fund 53

Pesh Valley 13, 73, 200, 201

Peshaei 6, 112, 113, 129

Peshawar 6, 25, 78, 104, 112, 129, 141, 202

Popal, IDLG Director Ghulam Jalani 162

Provincial Reconstruction Teams (PRTs) xv, 8, 18, 27, 28, 34, 38, 39, 44, 48, 50, 51, 52, 54, 59, 62, 67, 71, 72, 73, 76, 77

RC-East (Regional Command-East) xiv, xxi, 1, 4–11, 17–20, 23, 27–29, 31–32, 35–39, 43–44, 47, 49–60, 63–64, 66–67, 69, 71–72, 75–76, 83, 85, 87–89, 92–93, 95, 100, 102–4, 107, 135–42, 145, 149–56, 177, 194, 196, 199, 202, 204

RC-South 48, 48, 83, 138, 170

Regional Afghan Municipalities Program for Urban Populations (RAMP-UP) 166

Rule of Law (ROL) programs 17, 113, 116, 137

Sarobi, Governor Habiba 32, 205

Special Representative for Afghanistan and Pakistan (SRAP) 66, 83, 92

Salafist 9, 127

Salerno, Forward Operating Base 71, 83

Sharan 71, 193, 200, 201, 202

Sherzai, Governor Gul Agha 116, 117, 119

shuras 58, 88, 166

Soviets 2, 5, 8, 32, 36, 75, 107, 112, 127, 128, 130, 131, 132, 133, 142, 150, 156, 189

Supreme Court 163, 216

Tajiks 6, 26, 33, 83, 87, 129, 140, 146, 150, 199

Taliban 2, 3, 5, 8, 9, 20, 23, 24, 25, 26, 31, 32, 33, 35, 37, 41, 47, 52, 55, 60, 61, 72, 76, 84, 88, 89, 90, 91, 93, 94, 96, 113, 118, 121, 122, 128, 129, 130, 131, 132, 133, 134, 136, 138, 139, 140, 142, 143, 146, 151, 154, 170, 182, 185, 186, 197, 203, 204, 205, 208, 213, 214

Taniwal, Governor Hakim 32, 89, 130

Task Force Bayonet 72, 73, 74, 196

Torkham Gate 74, 83, 103, 104, 114

U.S. Department of Agriculture (USDA) xvii, 28, 52, 63, 71, 74, 92, 155, 180, 202, 205

United Nations Assistance Mission in Afghanistan (UNAMA) 18, 19, 29, 31, 55, 130, 131, 141, 163, 171, 181, 186, 194, 195, 197

United Nations High Commissioner for Refugees 194

US Agency for International Development (USAID) 27, 47–68, 84, 87, 91, 96, 115, 120, 162, 164, 166, 167, 168, 180, 183, 194, 202, 205

US Forces – Afghanistan (USFOR-A) 167, 172

Wahhabist 9, 24
Wahidi, Governor Fazlullah 32, 41, 125
Wardak Province 67, 69, 90, 91, 196
Waziristan 15, 24, 25, 37, 67, 102, 105, 175, 176, 192, 193

wolesi jirga 15
World Bank 34, 53, 155, 183

Zadran Arc Initiative 194
Zadran tribe 26, 139, 194

www.ingramcontent.com/pod-product-compliance
Lightning Source LLC
Chambersburg PA
CBHW020752160426
43192CB00006B/314